PRAISE FOR SELL

"Finka's book absolutely transformed the way I approach selling and marketing. Her ideas and techniques - and most of all her transmission of confidence and yes, love - will change how you sell forever. Read this book and then put it to work for you."

Jennifer Louden, best-selling author of
Why Bother? Discover the Desire for What's Next

"This is a read right now book! Finka answers why we have a growing resistance to fear based selling. She provides an irresistible and practical framework that tosses fear to the curb and opens our hearts to embracing wholehearted and sustainable growth. This book will revitalize you, and your business – as love does! Prepare to be transformed!"

Janet Lee, CEO and Founder The Story Co.

"I could not put *Sell From Love* down. At first it felt uncomfortable to think about 'love' and 'selling', but you quickly realize the examples and practical tools make so much sense. This is a necessary read for anyone dealing with sales and relationships and isn't just for your clients - this will transform you personally. As a leader the takeaways and understanding you will gain to manage a team are unlimited. Finka, you are a trail blazer!"

Sheri Griffiths, Senior Vice President,
Head of Ontario, Canadian Commercial Banking

"*Sell From Love* provides a fresh perspective and practical tips on how to be a successful sales professional in today's business world. Finka takes a holistic approach to sales, focusing first on "love yourself", and ultimately proving you can be a good person, do good work and make money doing it. I highly recommend this book for sales professionals and sales leaders alike."

Doug Palmer, Former Regional President Business Banking,
Bank of Montreal

"For those of us who care about others and want to make a meaningful difference in the world, *Sell From Love* is the heart-centered sales strategy we've been searching for. Practical examples and engaging stories bring the book's simple processes to life, demonstrating a clear path to natural and fulfilling client relationships. Jerkovic practices what she teaches, making this work authentic, powerful, and effective."

Andrea Joy Wenburg, M.A., author, speaker, and founder of the Voice of Influence® consulting agency and podcast

"*Selling from Love* may sound like a soft approach, but it is actually a roadmap of the rigorous work of building inner trust while illuminating the path to moving from transaction to transformation—of yourself, your story, your way of showing up, and your performance. Whether you're a seasoned sales professional or a new solopreneur who dreads sales, you'll find this rich and substantive book an inspiring guide to the satisfaction and sustainability that come from being true to yourself and wholly aligned with what you bring to the world."

Gail Larsen, author of *Transformational Speaking: If You Want to Change the World, Tell a Better Story* (Random House and Brilliance Audio)

"I have read almost every sales book you can possibly imagine. You name it, I've probably read it. Finka's book *Sell From Love* offers a totally different perspective on selling than everything else out there. In the book, she helps you to remove what is stopping you in your sales game so you can become much more effective for you, your business and, most importantly, those you serve. For anyone who is looking to improve their sales and make a difference, *Sell From Love* offers a new perspective that changes the paradigm of how selling should be. If you are someone who has a message, wants to make an impact, and wants to make more sales, you need to start selling from love. And this book gives you the step by step instructions on how to do just that!"

David Keesee, author,
The Find A Way Book, creator of The Find A Way Code
30,000+ TRAINED | 3,000+ COACHED | 15X RESULTS

"*Sell From Love* is a labor of love. Finka simply guides the reader through changing the focus from fear to love. This allows a salesperson or anyone, for that matter, to focus on all the right things about the client-salesperson interaction. Instead of being adversarial, the sales process becomes transformational. This complete step-by-step model helps anyone shift the sales process from being a fearful burden to one of grace and elegance."

Susan Stageman, M.A. President, NLP Training Concepts, LLC, Master Practitioner/ Master Certified Trainer, Society of Neurolinguistic Programming

"Just as the world turned upside down and business leaders were forced to adapt to new ways of approaching work, *Sell From Love* came in like a beacon of light. Finka's thoughtful, practical, and inspirational process is exactly what is needed to keep driving results while also remaining conscious of how we go about obtaining those results. Spending endless hours sleepwalking through business, fueled by the fear of failure, is a thing of the past. When you embrace your distinct value, approach clients from a place of genuine service, and believe your offer will solve your clients' problems, you can sell from a place of love, not fear. It is a welcome ideology refresh for strategically selling products, services, and even ideas, which is why now, more than ever, *Sell From Love* is needed in businesses worldwide."

Amber Hurdle, author, speaker, podcast host, and CEO of Amber Hurdle Consulting

"*Sell From Love* will give you the courage to consistently show up for your clients every day. Finka helps readers identify the barriers and fears that get in their own way and provides real insights, actionable ideas, and helpful exercises to help any entrepreneur find their Brilliant Difference and love for selling. The reality is today's business environment demands fresh ideas and perspectives. This book delivers and will empower you to sell in a new world!"

Sandra Corelli, founder and CEO, Humanicity Consulting Group

"LOVE THIS BOOK!! As a life-long entrepreneur it's easy to get caught up in "chasing the sale". Finka's *Sell From Love* philosophy reminded me that selling is an extension of who I am and how I can help people. The second I forget this, I end up with clients I don't want and dollars I'd rather not have. It's that simple. When you bring your best self to the table, you attract the right clients and your offer is a solution that solves their problem. It's the best feeling to live this way in my business."

Heather Korol, founder of Master Your Message,
author of *A Slice of Happy*.

"*Sell From Love* is a must-read for every entrepreneur! In this book, Finka Jerkovic takes you through her signature process and teaches you how to tap into your Brilliant Difference and think of sales in a totally different way. The book is packed full of powerful stories, examples, and takeaways that will help you sell (share your gifts with the world) from a deeper, more meaningful place. You'll not only walk away with a new perspective on sales, you'll have a powerful framework that will transform how you connect with potential clients and share the transformation you offer."

Laura Beauparlant, founder and creative director,
Lab Creative, author of Brand Chemistry

"With *Sell From Love*, Finka Jerkovic challenges all of our assumptions about sales and invites us into a more human, more creative approach to closing the deal. What's more, Finka's approach to sales helps us see ourselves with the capacity--even the responsibility--to make a truly positive impact on the people and communities we love. Oh, and it works, too."

Tara McMullin, founder of What Works

SELL
FROM
LOVE

ISBN 978-1-7773351-3-7 (hardcover)
ISBN 978-1-7773351-0-6 (paperback)
ISBN 978-1-7773351-4-4 (e-book)
ISBN 978-1-7773351-1-3 (audio)

Edited by Katie Zdybel
Proofread by Lise Gunby
Writing Coach Jennifer Louden
Cover Design Damonza Studio
Interior Design Indie Publishing Group

For more information visit www.sellfromlove.com

Jelena – You inspire me every day to be a better human.

Nick – For your commitment and saying yes to living out a full life.

I love you both with all my heart.

All of this is possible because of you.

Love is patient

love is kind

it does not envy

it does not boast

it is not proud

it is not rude

it is not self-seeking

it is not easily angered,

it keeps no record of wrongs

it does not delight in evil but rejoices with the truth

it always protects

always trusts

always hopes

always perseveres

Love never fails

1 Corinthians 13:4[1]

CONTENTS

—

SELL FROM LOVE

FINKA JERKOVIC

INTRODUCTION

—

"Love is the bridge between you and everything."

Rumi

MY MOUTH DROPPED open and my heart sank when I heard the VP of Sales say: "We need people who are hungry and who hustle, and we need to get rid of the fu*king rest." *Did he just say that?* I asked myself. I was rooted in place, disheartened and in utter disbelief.

He was referring to his company's more than two thousand dedicated employees who showed up every day to serve and manage the organization's highest and most valued clients.

It was a mid-November afternoon that I will never forget. Along with two hundred sales leaders, I was attending a national sales conference. This was an annual, motivational-strategy-deployment meeting. I was attending because I had been hired to coach many of the leaders in the room.

My first thought was, *wow, we are not on the same page. What about the humble and modest salespeople who aren't overtly salesy, over- the-top social and boisterous? What about the successful salespeople who don't schmooze to close deals?* These salespeople act differently and they're struggling because they don't fit into the traditional selling environment. They approach clients with a quiet presence. They bring an intention to serve their clients first and foremost, and to understand their needs. Instead of pushing the latest product on which their company will pay the most commissions, these salespeople focus on doing what's right for the client, even if it means a little less in their own bank account. They are hungry and they hustle—to do what's right and best for their clients.

Most clients are not looking for the loud, over-the-top, pushy salesperson. It's a turn-off. This hungry-and-hustle selling style has clients believing salespeople are more focussed on their own interests and the bottom line than on them and their bottom line. You can be hungry and you can hustle. But when it's motivated by fear, ego, self-interest, and self-preservation, this type of selling doesn't work. It's short-lived, soul-depleting, serves only one person—you—and it won't help you grow your business.

When selling is motivated from love instead of fear, it is built on a foundation of genuineness and humbleness. You put your clients' interests above yours; you listen to understand; you put yourself in their shoes; you use your knowledge, skills, and expertise to add value; you strive to bring solutions that will transform their lives.

Unfortunately, at this national sales conference, the old-school, sell-from-fear sales model was alive and well. This all-too-familiar outdated model does not work. It is a desperate way to do business, diminishes the credibility of both the buyer and the seller, and leaves in its wake a permanent residue of dissatisfaction. You know what it feels like when someone sells from fear: they're awkward, chaotic, and there never seems to be enough time to take advantage of their special offer. I recently received a promotional email that said, "Register now, before someone else does!" This is selling from fear. The special offer is staged in a manner that your decision to buy comes from FOMO (fear of missing out), rather than taking advantage of something you really want and need. There is a place for time-limited, special offers when selling. It's a valuable method to engage ideal clients, but not if the result instills more fear because of how you sell.

As a professional who sells products, services, and expertise, wouldn't you want to sell and buy differently? This disappointing conference event was exactly what I needed to motivate me to share my radical, and far more effective, alternative.

Selling From Love Lesson

I've been in sales for my entire career, first in corporate financial services and then as a business owner. In my banking days, I was an account manager and financial adviser for more than ten years, helping clients with business, lending, and investment advice and solutions. I loved this work. Most of all, I loved helping my clients solve problems and achieve their goals. I loved helping them buy their first home, increase cash flow to expand their business, or save for their once-in-a-lifetime European vacation. The mortgage, business line of credit, or mutual fund was just the tool we used to help get them there.

Later, with my sales experience, I moved into head office to support the bank's sales strategy and communications division and I was soon appointed as sales leader. I was no longer in charge of my performance alone; I was leading a sales team. Over the next fifteen years, I'd learn a lot about myself, my motivations, and my impact on others. When you become a leader, you're responsible for more than yourself. Your intentions, actions, and behaviors are under a microscope, and your impact and results are always in the spotlight. There's nowhere to hide—the good, the bad, and the ugly are always on display. This is where my ideas about selling from love started to emerge.

I was hired by a bank as a branch manager to lead one of their most high-profile branches in the heart of Toronto. They hired me for my unique perspective as I was coming from a different organization. I had a high-performing sales track record with numerous awards and accolades. Plus, my leadership style always had my teams trying new progressive ideas. The teams I led knew there was no shortage of ways I could come up with on how to improve, engage, and invite more clients to work with us. I studied and researched sales and marketing strategies that our competitors and non-related industry professionals used. I was excited to bring change, opportunity for growth, and connection to deeper and more meaningful work to this team and community. It was only about five months into the job that things started to change—and not for the better.

Results weren't happening fast enough and my boss, Ted, was feeling the pressure from the top. He was getting impatient with my approach, and fear and doubt were starting to set in. Fear that I wasn't going to turn this into a top-performing branch, and doubt that he had hired the right person for the job. Turning a ship takes time, patience, and commitment to a bigger vision and strategy. I had a plan and I knew it would work, but then I, too, started doubting myself. I questioned if my plan would really work and if my entire career was a fluke. I wondered if all those wins were only a façade, something I had made up. I was afraid.

I feared my job and career were at risk. At the same time, I knew that if my actions were motivated from a place of fear, I'd lose my authentic, true self, and I'd focus more on my results instead of serving others. Even in light of this knowing, in an environment flooded with fear, I decided the best, safest, and least risky option was to let go of what I knew to be true and to do it their way—or I should say, to sell from fear.

Ted pushed the micro-management sales method the company was accustomed to, which included checking in on my team *hourly* to see who they had called, what meetings they had had, and what products and services they had sold. When selling from love, professionals and leaders replace control and authority with trust, empathy, and service. To sell from love doesn't mean you don't track your sales processes and activities—you still do. The difference is that you're not focused on outcomes, nor are you attached to them. Instead, you're aligned to your intentions to bring your best self, to do good work, and to help others. You're keeping an eye on your sales activities—calls, meetings, and accepted invitations—from a place of curiosity, not control. You still want to sell because you are dedicated to being of service. You are not loyal to self-interest and fear.

I was working under this performance pressure cooker of control and micro-management for two weeks. It felt as though I was walking on eggshells, afraid if I made one wrong move, I'd be fired. It was a spring day and I was walking through the branch lobby towards the customer service desk.

I started feeling pain in my chest and my left arm went numb. I thought I was having a heart attack. I quickly ran to my office, grabbed my jacket and purse, and drove myself to the ER. I didn't tell a soul. I feared if anyone knew, they'd think I was too soft for the job and couldn't handle the pressure.

At the hospital, I was immediately wired up to the EKG. As I lay there, the monitor beeping, I was flooded with grief and sadness. *How did this happen? How did I let fear take over? Was being who I thought they wanted me to be going to cost me my life?* I was so far from my centre. I had lost my north star and vowed if I got out alive, I'd get myself back on track and re-aligned.

It wasn't a heart attack; it was a panic attack. However, to me, what it really was, was a warning sign. My actions were being motivated by fear—fear I'd not make my numbers, fear I'd fail, fear I'd disappoint my boss, and fear I'd lose my job. This fear was creating havoc in my team, instilling stress and disconnect and wasn't helping us get any closer to achieving our results. Even though it was scary to follow what I knew to be true, at this point it was scarier *not* to, because I knew what was at stake: everything that made me *me*.

The next day I was back in my office booking a meeting to break the news to my boss. I told Ted I was going to do it the way I had always done it, and that I was going to follow what I had known to be true. I reminded him that these were all the reasons he had hired me. If he accepted, I'd stay; and if not, I was out. I asked him to give me until the end of the year. I knew I could turn this branch around; I just needed more time. We had a candid conversation and he gave me back my branch and allowed me to lead it the way I knew best. And yes, it worked. The branch ended the year in the top 10%, a long way from the bottom where we started.

I knew there was a method to this way of selling, but I didn't yet know what it was called or how to quantify what I had done. Over the next eight years, as a leadership, sales, and branding coach working with more than ten thousand leaders, sales professionals and entrepreneurs, from Fortune 500 to large corporate and small business, I successfully developed and taught what I'd intuitively discovered. Sell from love is built on my more than two-decade career in sales and a foundation of research that includes 235 global interviews with entrepreneurs, financial advisers, coaches, consultants, and service-based professionals. In addition, I've participated in more than 800 coaching sessions, observing leaders directly coaching their sales teams. My role was to help them improve their sales coaching skills so that their teams could sell with confidence, build client loyalty, and grow the business.

It was right there; it was always there, all along, obvious as the sun in the day. But now I could finally see it. Have you ever had one of those moments when it feels like the clouds open up and the sun shines through, with angels singing "alleluia she finally got it!"? Well, that's what it was like.

The phrase that best captured this approach was 'sell from love'.

Selling from love is a business strategy unlike any other. You can be a good person, do good work, and make good money doing it. Selling from love will help you get more clients, grow your business, and make a meaningful impact on others.

Two Types of Selling

There are two ways to sell. You can sell from love or you can sell from fear. At any given time, you are selling in one of these two constructs. Selling from love looks seamless and feels like you're flowing downstream. It may not always be easy, but you walk away invigorated and energized, just like you feel after a good workout. When you sell from love you look like you— meaning you're not pretending to be someone you're not. You're authentic and you use your personality to connect with clients. When you sell from love, you're generous and you strive to give your clients the best options. Their interests come first. Selling from love doesn't mean that fear is not present at times; what it means is that you don't let it stop you from moving forward. Selling from love means you act with courage and non-attachment to a specific outcome. When you sell from love, your road to success is wide open, unscripted, and organic. You can look to others for best practices and ideas on how to sell better or more, but know that when you embrace this philosophy, it's a personal journey and a customized road to success. This framework is creative, steeped in abundance and has an expanded winner's circle. Selling from love is a win for your client, for you the professional, for your company, for the community you live and work in, and for the world.

Selling from fear, on the other hand, can look desperate and needy. Instead of ease and flow, you're frantic, awkward, and stumbling. Selling from fear is rushed and hurried: you need to close the sale quickly or rush the client through the selling process so you can hit your target by the end of the month. When selling from fear, you lack natural confidence, so either you're holding back because of doubt or you're overcompensating by being overconfident and coming across as the know-it-all expert. Selling from fear feels "salesy". It's that impression you don't want to experience or leave with your clients.

Consider the impact it has on your client. Selling from love lets your client know you care about them. They feel supported, understood, and they feel that you "get them". When you sell from fear your client feels like a number. They lose trust in you and this drives a wedge between you and clients. They feel confused and scared. When you sell from fear, clients sense it and that fear will permeate through your relationship. They'll feel hustled and pressured, and they may end up buying from fear. You don't want your clients to buy from fear. It will prevent you from building long-lasting relationships, creating advocates for your brand, and delivering a meaningful transformation. Fear buys transactions; love fulfills a transformation. When you sell from love, you've created the perfect *let's work together* invitation for your client.

I've got some good news and some bad news. Let's start with the bad news first. Your environment is filled with triggers that will provoke you to sell from fear: the global economy, scarcity and the accompanying worry that there's not enough to go around, FOMO, "comparisitis" due to social media, concerns of business drying up due to a recession or market change, thoughts swirling in your head that you're not enough or too much—all of these triggers incite you to sell from fear. But don't despair: you don't have to sell from fear. You have an alternative: you can choose to sell from love. Even in the midst of FOMO or comparisitis you have the power to choose to love yourself and feed yourself thoughts and feelings from your inner champion rather than your inner critic. Selling from fear will pull you into your past, regressing as you dwell on things that didn't go as planned. Or it will propel you into the future where you worry about where your next sale will come from or become stressed about an upcoming presentation. Selling from love lives only in one place, in the here and now. You are present, listening with a keen ear, focused on your clients, open with curiosity and wonder.

Ultimately, selling from love feels expansive and will allow you to live out your purpose and potential. It is a whole-hearted invitation to allow yourself to be open and receptive to receive all the gifts that are available.

Here's a quick snapshot of what it is like to sell from fear versus love:

Selling from fear is...	Selling from love is....
False	Authentic
Confused	Clear
Fearful	Courageous
Self-directed criticism	Self-directed compassion
Past or future-oriented	Present-oriented
Unfeeling	Empathetic
Transactional	Transformational
Unconscious	Conscious
Disconnected	Connected
Profit-driven	Purpose-fulfilling
Self-serving	Generous
Egotistic	Altruistic
Competitive	Cooperative
Not enough	More than enough
Indifferent	Loyal
Constricted or limited	Receptive or unlimited

Take a moment now to reflect personally on what selling from fear and selling from love is like for you. Grab a pen and notepad and respond to the following questions:

- What does selling from fear look like? What does selling from love look like?

- What does selling from fear feel like? What does selling from love feel like?

- What triggers moments of fear? What activates moments of love?

- What is the impact when you sell from fear on you? On your client?

- What is the impact when you sell from love on you? On your client?

You Need to Sell From Love

The market, the economy, and the consumer are changing, and so is humanity. Who we are today and, more importantly, who we need to be tomorrow, is evolving. There is a movement toward more conscious and sustainable business practices focused not only on profit, but on individuals, community, and the environment. We've made a real mess of our planet and we need to repair and replenish what has been damaged. More businesses are endeavoring to become sustainable or green. For example, the B Label Certification distinguishes companies that achieve sustainability by balancing profit and purpose[1].

How we sell our products, offer our services, and conduct our expertise is part of this evolution. The traditional method—the always-be-closing, crushing-quota method—not only adds to the stressful discomfort of pushy selling, but contributes to a competitive, fear-based environment in the marketplace. These traditional methods tightly link the purpose of a business to rewarding the few, specifically the shareholders. Regardless of the cost to the environment, resources, employees, and customers, profit and shareholder interests take precedence.

What the world needs today is a more conscious, compassionate, and caring sales model, one that is based on authenticity, empathy, service—and yes, love. Selling from love not only feels good, it'll help you get clients, sell better, and make money selling your products and services while making a positive impact in the world.

I want to offer you three reasons why you should sell from love so that you too can benefit from a sales approach that is:

- conscious and compassionate about you the salesperson,

- empathetic and understanding about your clients and their needs and priorities and,

- mindful and purposeful about the impact you have on the environment you live and work in.

Reason #1: Selling from love will teach you how to love yourself

People don't want to be sold to, they don't want a salesperson, they want you. They want you to show up as a real, genuine, authentic human. People see through inauthenticity when you're being someone you're not. This will cost you clients, sales, and revenue.

Being who you truly are is scary, especially when you're putting yourself out there, networking, selling, and marketing yourself, your products or services. You worry if you embrace and truly own your strengths, talents, and expertise. You worry that you'll be perceived as self-centred, as having a big ego, or as being over-the-top and too much. Or you might be stressing about your weaknesses, what you don't know or what you've not yet achieved, feeling as though you don't know enough, don't have enough experience, or that you're not good enough.

Our brains are wired to keep us safe. Devaluing, dismissing, and denying who you really are is the work of fear. Bringing out the strengths, talents, knowledge, and expertise you bring to the table can be scary. Bringing out your authentic self makes you vulnerable and puts your true self at risk for judgement, criticism and, worst of all, rejection. People may not like you, may not want you, or may not want what you're selling. All of this is risky business for your brain, and it will do whatever it can to keep you safe, even if it means hiding who you really are behind a suit of armor.

You were not born to be a sales professional. These are skills you develop. For instance, you may be an introvert; growing up, maybe you were quite shy. You look at your colleagues and compare your observant, quiet, thoughtful approach and decide it doesn't measure up to who you need to be to sell. What if selling from love allowed you not only to use your introvert skills to your advantage, but also helped you fall in love with yourself even more because of it?

Fear reacts and love responds. Neuroplasticity experts tell us that we can rewire our brains, that the default fight, flight, or freeze fear reaction is something we can teach our brains to respond to differently.

When you sell from love, you'll learn how to create an environment where you make it safe for your brain to sell and market your products, services, and expertise. When you sell from love, you'll learn how to show up by being you, no matter how different or unique you are. Selling from love invites you to let go of who you think you need to be in order to be successful and instead embrace who you already are by bringing your special gifts, talents, and expertise to the table.

This means that when you're getting ready to post an article on LinkedIn, pick up the phone to call a warm lead, or ask a client to work with you, instead of hesitating, holding back or doing it in a way that's not fully aligned to your true self, you move forward, taking action with courage, confidence, and integrity, loving yourself no matter what the outcome may be.

Reason #2: Selling from love will teach you how to love your client

The second reason you need to sell from love is for your clients. Your clients have changed. They're no longer looking for transactions to satisfy them. They want more; they want a transformation. It's not about the mortgage they're getting; it's about the dream home with the perfect kitchen for family get-togethers they can enjoy because of the mortgage. It's not about the massage therapy; it's about the flexibility they gain, so they can play with their grandkids. It's not about the counsel you provide on their investment portfolio; it's about the freedom and peace of mind they get to have because they've invested wisely. The mortgage, the massage, the advice—these are the transactions you use to facilitate a transformation for your clients.

What's changed is that your clients need you to love them so much that you make the transaction you're selling secondary and put the transformation they're receiving at the forefront of everything you do.

The transaction is focused more on you, your product and service, not your client. It's the tool you use to facilitate a transformation for your client. The transaction doesn't define the change your client will have, the transformation does. The transformation is the promise they can expect and the experience they get as a result of the transaction you are selling.

Often, as professionals, we can get stuck in the product details, features and benefits and, worst of all, price. This is the transactional conversation. This is important, but it can't be centre stage, especially when selling from love. According to a study done by Accenture, 77% of buyers believe that salespeople don't understand their business[2]. This means that we're so focused on what we're selling that we forget who we're selling to, or rather, who's buying from us.

Today, with a few clicks on Google, your potential and current clients find transactions easily. What they want is a transformation. They want to know how you can make their problems go away, help them achieve their goals, honor their values, and fulfill their dreams. They need you to love them that much, so that you're more invested in the transformation they get and not the transaction you sell.

Reason #3: Selling from love will teach you how to love your offer

The world is changing and it's changing fast. The state of humanity, the climate, consciousness, and the rapid growth of digitalization, virtual working environments, and artificial intelligence is inviting each of us to step up and be the change the world needs right now. What the world needs now is more purpose, empathy, connection, authenticity, courage, and love. What the world needs most is for you to be the mechanism that delivers it.

I believe that you've been put on this planet for a reason. You have someone you need to be, something to do, and an experience to have. You have a purpose to fulfill. Selling from love means that, whether you're an entrepreneur, business owner, consultant, leader, or sales professional in an organization, you use the work you do, the clients you serve, the products, services, and expertise you bring, as a way to deliver on your purpose.

In a study conducted by PwC, 79% of business leaders surveyed believe that an organization's purpose is central to their business success, yet 68% reported that purpose is not used as a guidepost in leadership decision-making processes within their organization[3].

What that means is that not only does it feel good to do purposeful work, it makes business sense to use your business to deliver on your purpose, and indeed it will contribute to your success.

Having a purpose and living it out is also important to your clients and teams. With 75% of millennials making up the workforce and earning power, they are 5.3 times more likely to stay with an organization if they have a strong connection to their purpose[4]. Whether you're hiring sales professionals to work in your company, a sales leader or an entrepreneur, having a strong purpose will help you create connection and attract the right employees and clients to your organization and team.

When seeking advice, 77% of consumers will choose a human over a digital capability[5]. This is great news. Today there's very little differentiation between many products and services in the market. It's either a commodity or it's well on its way to becoming one. There may be a few features and a price on your solutions that you can use to differentiate yourself; however, this only focuses on the transactional side of your offer and isn't a good growth strategy.

What's going to differentiate you, help you attract your ideal clients, and make the work you do feel authentic and aligned, is bringing more of you. It's the advice, expertise, experience, ideas, insights, personality, and thought leadership you bring to the table, that will differentiate you and move your client's experience from a transaction to a transformation. Selling from love invites us to use our personality to humanize the transaction. Even with the increase in digitalization in the world today, we make it a point to bring the human touch in all that we do.

When selling from love, your offer is a means to actualize on the deeper, more meaningful reason and purpose to your life. Your purpose is not to sell a mortgage, massage therapy, or a new home. This offer helps you deliver the positive impact and meaningful change you're here to make in this world. When you understand that your products, services, and expertise are the vehicle you use to allow you to bring peace of mind, nourish families, and empower voices, you know you're selling from love.

A Personal Love Note

My wish for you is that you accept this invitation to use the insights, tools and resources in this book to sell from love. The ripple effect we will create together will give rise to a world that loves more and fears less. Where authenticity, empathy, connection, courage and love abound. By loving who you are fully and unconditionally, by understanding your clients, and by using your work and selling as a means to deliver on your purpose, your life, your business and the world will be transformed.

You don't have to do this alone. I've created some additional resources for you to supplement your reading and support you along your journey to sell from love.

First, the Sell From Love Test. This is a diagnostic tool to help you assess where you are and where you're not selling from love. You'll quickly uncover what areas are key for you to focus on, so you can sell with more authenticity, create transformations for your clients, and find more meaning, impact, and success when selling your ideas and services. You can take the Sell From Love Test at www.sellfromlove.com/test to learn where your selling gap is and where your biggest opportunity lies:

- Do you need to love yourself?

- Do you need to love your client?

- Do you need to love your offer?

Next, the Sell From Love Workbook. This book is filled with practical, immediately implementable ideas and solutions. This book is not theory. This book is designed to help you take the insights and ideas shared here and apply them directly to your leadership and business. Throughout the book I've included real-life examples and exercises that will help you learn how to love yourself, love your client, and love your offer. You can download the Sell From Love Workbook at www.sellfromlove/workbook to help you apply the sell-from-love methodology to your sales and marketing practices.

Finally, the Sell From Love Community. Putting yourself out there, selling and marketing your products, services, and expertise, running a business, and standing up in your leadership takes courage, conviction, and commitment. You don't need to go it alone. That's why I've created the Sell From Love Community. This is a collective of like-minded and like-spirited leaders, business owners, and change makers, who are devoted to changing the game of traditional selling and marketing practices. This community is here to support you to implement your ideas, stay consistent, and remain dedicated to your commitment to sell from love. You can join the Sell From Love Community at www.sellfromlove.com/community to help you stay anchored and connected and to continue learning how to sell from love.

Are you ready? Let's dive in!

PART ONE:

—

LOVE YOURSELF

CHAPTER ONE:
FALL IN LOVE WITH YOU

—

"To be yourself in a world that is constantly trying to make you something else is the greatest accomplishment."

Ralph Waldo Emerson

B E WHO YOU are so you can become who you're here to be. I wish I had known this when I was six years old. It was a sunny September morning and the first day of grade one. My mom and I were heading to the school office to register me at my new school. I was nervous, excited, and eager to meet new friends and start school. As we walked through the corridor doors, she looked down at me and said, "Finka, do you want to change your name?"

"Change my name?" I replied, with surprise. With good intention, she said, "Yes, to make it easier on yourself." When I was growing up, names like Mary, Lisa, and Cathy were the norm. Finka was different. This was my first lesson on difference, namely that when there is something different about you, you need to change it to fit in. I stood there in the school hall for a moment. What name would I choose? The only name that I could think of was Josie.

It wasn't a random name; it was my babysitter's daughter's name. Josie was twelve and my six-year-old self wanted to be everything she was. I wanted to style my hair like hers and wear the off-the-shoulder, flower-print, flowy dresses that had a perfume to match. Josie was perfect and, if I was like her, then I would be perfect too.

This was my chance. I looked up at my mom and said, "I want to be called Josie!" And she registered me as Josie. That was the start of how I learned to change my differences *supposedly* to make life easier for me. It might have felt easier in the moment, but over the long haul it would cost me.

At home I was Finka. At school and later in my corporate career, I was Josie. I lived a dual life. One version of me at home and another version of me at work. I sliced and diced my personality. At home, I was easy-going, playful, and creative; at work, I was ambitious, competitive, and results-oriented.

Based on the situation, I'd determine which story, personality trait, or skillset would be best suited. If it was too different or I'd stand out, I'd hold back. If my ideas or opinions would challenge the status quo, I'd hesitate or back down quickly, avoiding conflict and attention. Because of the tension caused by thinking differently, I deemed it to be wrong and unacceptable. Indeed, at times we need to hold back and look to bring peace rather than conflict to a situation. However, what was integral here was that my actions were being motivated from a place of fear, fear that I would not be accepted if I brought who I was.

Self-doubt Is Fueled by Fear that Stops You From Thriving

Not only was I hiding who I was, I was doubting that what I did was of any value. I was my own worst critic. I could have named countless ways to discount, dismiss, and devalue myself. I could have told you the many things I wasn't good at, couldn't do, and struggled with. I could also have given you a list of what was wrong, broken, and didn't measure up in myself. I'd spent an inordinate amount of time in my life and career proving, pleasing, perfecting, and pushing myself to perform and meet expectations.

All this discounting, dismissing, and devaluing only filled me with doubt. When you doubt yourself, your value, or your products and services, you create doubt with your clients. This doubt will cripple your sales and leadership because your clients will believe about you what you believe about yourself. For instance, this lack of confidence would show up in my client meetings. When making a recommendation I'd say something like "Perhaps you'd like to consider this as an option" or "I think maybe this would probably work for you." This tentative language allowed me to play it safe. I wasn't picking a concrete position, which gave me room to go where the wind blew, in case they didn't agree. My safety contributed to my clients' indecision and only added uncertainty to their situation. They came to me for help and all I helped them know was that I was uncertain.

The doubt and fear of being my authentic self was causing me pain and limiting my potential. It was standing in the way of becoming who I was meant to be. I wasn't bringing all of me, all of the time. I knew what alignment felt like and the happiness, success, and fulfillment I experienced when I brought my true self to my work and my clients. I also knew very well what dissonance felt like; even with outer success (sales ranking, awards, and promotions), I knew the feeling of unhappiness, frustration, and dissatisfaction that could go along with it.

Pushing down who you are by pushing out who you think you need to be takes a lot of energy and effort. It was exhausting. Looking back at it today, I can see this was a key contributor to ending up in the ER that spring day.

Selling From Love Starts with Falling in Love with You

"You wander room to room. Hunting for the diamond necklace. That is already around your neck."

Rumi

It was the summer of 2012, a few short months after my panic attack. In my inbox landed an invitation to take a free personality test. The test was called How to Fascinate® created by New York Times bestselling author Sally Hogshead. It was a quick test—five minutes—that would change the trajectory of my life forever. The results of the test were meant to show you how the world sees you at your best. The test pinpoints which of your personality and communication traits impresses and influences others best.

My results told me I was a Trendsetter. My top two advantages were Innovation and Prestige. I'm all about game-changing ideas, challenging the status quo, and delivering with excellence. This profile was bang on. I finally remembered my gifts! The gifts I'd been dismissing, denying, and overlooking were right in front of me in my fifteen-page report.

If you've ever taken a personality test, you will know the "aha" you experience you can have when you get those results. The words in those pages are like a mirror. You feel seen, heard, and understood. It's important that you take this next step and find evidence in your work and life that demonstrate the characteristics, qualities, and traits these tests illuminate for you. If you don't find examples in your work and life that show how these traits show up in your day-to-day, as quickly as they shined a light on your gifts, they will swiftly leave and end up being only a flicker of light in your experience.

When I was a sales leader, I often found myself suggesting and implementing strategies and tactics that no one else was doing. I was a branch manager at the time, and we had an incredible offer for a mortgage campaign. My team proactively reached out to clients, making calls and talking to everyone who visited the branch. But we had no means, other than the national TV commercials the bank was airing, to reach the members of our local community who didn't bank with us. In a matter of days, we had flyers printed and delivered door-to-door to the neighborhood residents, inviting them to visit our branch to learn more about this special offer. Our team set up a first-time home buyers' educational seminar with a local real estate agent, lawyer, financial planner, and our mortgage advisers. This created buzz and excitement for our team and community. The campaign ended and we grew our business and had the largest mortgage sales ever in the history of this branch. Not only did we grow, we helped a whole lot more people. Clients who didn't deal with us, and who didn't know about us or our offer, now had an opportunity to take advantage of this offer and to work with a team that would always have them in mind as they tried new, creative, and innovative ways to serve them. Eventually these ideas were adopted and became the norm for other branches in our area too.

Taking this test reminded me of the 'trendsetting' ideas I brought to the table. I felt a strong connection to the essence of who I was, I knew that this was me and it was the good stuff I was meant to bring out in my work, life, and relationships.

Now I want you to picture a Trendsetter in a *bank*. Exactly! I finally understood why I felt like a square peg trying to fit into a round hole my entire career. If I had worked in the arts or in design, I'm sure my trendsetter mindset would have been appreciated differently. At the bank, we take care of people's money, so it's understandable why everyone leans toward the tried and true. I can't tell you how often I would pitch an idea and the uniform response would be heads shaking no, saying "no, we don't do it that way here; we've never done it that way before; no, it can't be done." That was the standard response. The impact of this had me internalizing and making up stories in my head that my ideas weren't good enough, that they were wrong and stupid, which eventually led me to believe something was wrong with me and that I wasn't good enough to be in that room.

Understanding my true gifts, through Fascinate®, meant the search was over; the diamond I was looking for was already in my pocket. I took this newfound discovery and began bringing more of me to my work. I felt a deeper connection to the work I was doing and my purpose for doing it. I now knew I was there to bring new ideas, challenge the way things had been done, and provide transformational solutions to the problems my team, company, and clients were facing. When they said no, I no longer took it personally. What I realized was that the way I was communicating my ideas wasn't always working. It wasn't that my ideas were wrong or bad, it's that they met the world differently, through their own unique Brilliant Difference. This meant I needed to get better at communicating my ideas.

My brain is wired in a way that goes from A to Z quickly. At times I can lose my audience on the way, as they don't see how I connected the dots from A to B to C. They need details, details I miss and sometimes forget to consider because my brilliance goes after the big idea. I will also add, even though I have some pretty darn good ideas, what makes them great is the ability to collaborate with everyone else's Brilliant Difference. It's when everyone gets to bring their own Brilliant Difference that we all get to shine. In Chapter 8, "Speak your client's love language", we'll talk more about these different ways to communicate so you can better connect, understand, and communicate your Brilliant Difference with your clients.

Selling from love invites you to fall in love with yourself and your brilliance. This brilliance is different from everyone else's, which means not everyone will understand or love it. What matters is that *you* know it and you appreciate it. In addition, this brilliance, which may be buried somewhere inside you, is here to add value, to make a difference, and give your life purpose and meaning.

Remember the story I shared with you earlier about changing my name? This was a crucial decision I made when I was six years old that rippled through my life for many years. I denied a big part of me and something that was different: my name.

A few years ago, I was attending an outdoor music festival with friends and we were talking about names and the meanings behind them. I was curious as to what Finka meant. I Googled it, and this is what the webpage displayed:

Finka - Gender Feminine. Usage: Croatian.

Diminutive: Jozefina

Related Names: Josefa, Josephine, Jozefien, Jo, Joetta, Josephina and Josie[1]

At six years old, I had picked a name that was the exact translation of my Croatian name! I felt as though I was in the twilight zone. I learned two lessons from this:

1. I sure was an intuitive six-year-old!

2. I thought I was on a journey to be who I thought I needed to be; however, my journey led me back to who I already was. I only needed to remember.

Your Brilliant Difference is the Key to Overcoming Fear and Conquering Self-doubt

Selling from love starts with falling in love with you. This package of you-ness that you're being invited to discover, claim, and fall in love with, is your Brilliant Difference. Your Brilliant Difference is made up of two parts:

Part 1) Your Brilliance. This is a compilation of your talents, gifts, personality, skills, knowledge, and experience. Your Brilliance is unique to you and is different from your competitor's and everyone else in your field.

Part 2) It's here to make a difference. This brilliant, unique, distinct package of "you-ness" is here to add value and make a meaningful difference to those you live and work with.

Look at your Brilliant Difference as the perfect solution to your ideal client's problem. It's the way to capture who you are, what makes you different, what you do best, who you serve, the problems you solve, and the results you deliver, all in one place. This provides you with a clear path to sell from love. Ultimately, your Brilliant Difference allows you to package and present who you are to whom you're ideally set up to work with.

When you create your personal brand and business around your Brilliant Difference you will feel more confident. It will differentiate you in the marketplace. It will help you attract and engage more clients and, as a result, close more sales and grow your business.

When you find your Brilliant Difference and love yourself for it, you know it's here to serve and has a bigger purpose. Your Brilliant Difference asks you to truly love who you are with no desire to be other than you. You accept who you are and who you're not. There's a sense of peace and contentedness that comes alongside being your authentic self. Identifying your Brilliant Difference will connect you to your essence and will grant you the confidence to put yourself out there to promote and sell yourself, your products, and services. Selling from love comes more naturally because you're being you.

Your Brilliant Difference is the special gift you bring to make the world a better place. It is your unique contribution to making a positive dent in the universe. Loving yourself helps you discover the meaning and purpose behind your work and life because you uncover your "why". Your Difference is the impact you're here to make on the people you're here to serve; it also creates motivation for you to bring more of you to your work. If you don't bring your Brilliant Difference, the world will never get to see its impact. Since nobody else has what you have, there's a real cost, to you and those you serve and love, in hiding your true self behind who you think you're supposed to be.

Falling in love with you is key to having a happy, fulfilling, and successful life. Falling in love with who you really are is fundamental to having the ability to sell from love. When you love yourself fully, you also learn to accept who you're not. There are things you don't know, are not good at, and don't like doing. You realize you're not perfect for everyone and everything. A relief comes with that because you no longer need to be someone you're not. Falling in love with you means you fall in love with your strengths by showing up fully, using them to serve. It also means acknowledging your weaknesses and not forcing yourself to learn skills you're less adept at. You're okay with the fact that you're not good at everything and you realize that you can't be everything to everyone because you need to be something to someone.

How do you discover your Brilliant Difference? You need to do some homework. Now, remember it comes so easily and naturally to you that you may not think it's such a big deal—hence, you've been missing it. It's also different from others, so most likely you've been discounting its value. Don't let this stop you. Your Brilliant Difference is what makes you a big deal and it's what will help you close deals.

The Impact of Gaining Clarity About Your Brilliant Difference

I got clear on how I wanted to express my Brilliant Difference. I wanted to coach, teach, and mentor passionate, ambitious change-makers. I wanted to deliver breakthrough transformations. Transactional, band-aid, short-sighted fixes are not my thing. "Go deep or go home" is my motto. I can do transactional, and it has its place; however, my mission is to help people go from transactional to transformational solutions and results.

I recall one sales leader I was coaching named Chris. He managed a team of account managers and I was there to help him improve his client loyalty scores and sales performance through coaching. Once a week, Chris, one of his account managers, and I would hop on a call together. Chris would coach his employee and I'd stand back to listen and observe to see how he used his coaching skills. When the session was complete, the employee would hang up and Chris and I would debrief on what worked, and what didn't work, during his coaching call.

Coaching sessions with leaders and employees can often look more like a tell and provide direction to employees meeting. The employee has a problem and the leader tells him or her what to do and how to fix it. This is transactional coaching, a trap many leaders, including myself, have fallen into.

By contrast, transformational coaching looks like this: listening, asking open-ended, curious questions, and holding back from telling employees what to do by instead inviting them to come up with their own solutions. This type of coaching requires a sales leader to be self-aware and have the ability to manage emotions and the ongoing narrative in their head, and to learn how to resist jumping in to save and solve.

Chris was falling into the transactional coaching trap. In our debriefs, we explored what was motivating Chris to jump in, tell, and direct; we also explored what held him back from pausing and allowing his employees to come up with their own solutions.

Chris had his breakthrough.

I asked him what he was afraid of. He replied, "I'm afraid if I don't tell them what to do or how to do it, they won't know." To which I followed-up, "And if that happened, what would happen next?"

He then went further, "They won't know what to do, they'd upset clients, decrease our client loyalty scores, lose sales, and would not perform. Then our team results would be affected, and I could get a poor rating and no bonus. Worse—eventually, I could lose my job."

Chris was not afraid of his employees not knowing what to do. Underneath it all, he jumped in to tell and direct his employees because he was afraid that if they didn't deliver, it would affect their performance, client experience and, one day, possibly cost him his job.

This realization was the first part of Chris's breakthrough. This was a Friday afternoon and I sent him home with some weekend homework. I asked him to think about this: "What would be the worst thing to happen if you didn't tell and direct your team?"

First thing Monday morning, Chris gave me a call. He said he had it. He had spent the weekend pondering this question and all the fears that had him showing up as a transactional coach. He desperately wanted to be the transformational leader he envisioned himself to be. He shared his reflections on his worst-case scenario:

"If I stopped telling and giving them the answers, they'd need to figure it out on their own. They may get it right, wrong, and even better solutions than any option I could provide them. If I would lose my job, that'd mean I'd lose my pay, my house and end up moving to our family beach house on the east coast. That doesn't seem so bad, after all."

Chris examined his fears, the possible worst that could happen, and reckoned he could handle it. This was the breakthrough he needed to uncover what was holding him back from being the best coach and leader he could be. This was his transformation.

Today, whether in corporate or as a business owner, my mission is to help leaders and professionals make a meaningful impact through their Brilliant Difference. Using what makes you unique to make you successful is the cornerstone of how I help my clients. I believe that when you get you right and fall in love with who you are, you'll have the clarity and confidence in your worth, you'll gain support and influence for your ideas, create both impact and recognition as a leader or expert in your field, and use your personal strengths to grow your business. This is what selling from love is all about and that is the transformation I am committed to creating with you.

And let me tell you, when you find your Brilliant Difference and fall in love with you, it ripples into other areas of your life: your personal relationships, hobbies and interests, lifestyle, health, and financial and spiritual wellbeing. I was well on my way to living in my Brilliant Difference through my work by building a coaching and training business focused on leadership, branding, sales and marketing, when I realized I wanted to live differently.

I was born and bred a city girl but longed for a more nature-based life. After a long, contemplative process, my husband, daughter, and I decided to sell our city life and move to the country. We moved to the country to live, work, and play on eighty-five acres. Today we grow most of our own vegetables, raise chickens, keep bees, and ride horses. We also planted a lavender field and make lavender essential oils, salts, and soaps. If I hadn't started to own my Brilliant Difference, I wouldn't be here living this lifestyle and doing this work.

Your Brilliant Difference is what will inform and influence who you are here to become. Doing this work and living this lifestyle were not even on my radar until I owned my Brilliant Difference. My business has grown, and attracting ideal clients and selling from love using my Brilliant Difference comes with ease, flow, and, dare I say, fun. I know I'm not a fit for everyone and not everyone is a fit for me and that's okay. I no longer feel the need to please, prove, be perfect, or perform to meet expectations because when I sell from love these impulses don't show up.

This is possible for you. Selling doesn't have to be hard or icky and it doesn't have to feel inauthentic. When you sell from love, using your Brilliant Difference, you'll be in awe of how easy it is. You'll wonder why it took you so long to get there.

Three Barriers Standing in the Way to Loving Yourself

Discovering and claiming your Brilliant Difference has its challenges. However, to set you up for success it's always best to be aware of the obstacles that will stand in the way of your discovering, claiming, and creating a business and life around your Brilliant Difference.

Barrier # 1: Your Brilliant Difference is unknown to you

Your innate gifts, the special skills, talents and that thing you're so brilliant at comes so easily and naturally to you, you don't even notice it and you will take it for granted. You're so close to what you're good at that it's hard for you to see it. You naturally understand others because you're empathetic, or you have an ability to deliver difficult information with elegance, or you come up with cutting edge insights after reviewing data and information. It's like you can't see the forest from the trees because you're the forest. As a result, you overlook this special, brilliant gift you bring.

This stops you from selling from love because you're not being who you really are. Selling from love means that you fully own who you are. Discovering your Brilliant Difference is work that's intentional. Your Brilliant Difference is inside of you, and you need to work to dig it up consciously. You need to find those parts that are invisible to you and make them visible.

Barrier # 2: Your brain is wired with a negativity bias

The human brain is wired to look at everything and anything that may pose a threat to you. It surveys your environment and picks up on any potential red flags. Whether you're being faced by a saber-toothed tiger or you just walked into a networking event, the feeling of fear instilled is the same. Negativity bias not only scans your external environment, it also focuses on what's wrong with you, what you don't have, or to whom you're not measuring up. It's always looking for what's wrong in order to protect you, so it distorts and limits your view of yourself as it only puts your attention on the negative.

This stops you from selling from love because your brain puts your attention on what's wrong with you instead of what's right. It will move you away from loving yourself because you'll be focused on reasons why you shouldn't love yourself. Selling from love requires you once again to be conscious of when your brain's negativity bias is taking you away from your Brilliant Difference.

Barrier # 3: Your attention is immersed in the tornado vortex

We live in a noisy, busy, distracted world. Attention is a finite resource. You're constantly being pulled in different directions and being diverted from your agenda and goals. So many things are vying for your attention: social media, your inbox, access to information overload, meetings, and everyone around you. This tornado moves you away from your Brilliant Difference, keeping you preoccupied on social media, looking at what your competitors are doing, or in your inbox replying to requests your administrator should be dealing with. You get held back in the office with no time to promote and present your Brilliant Difference to prospective clients.

This stops you from selling from love because you're focused on everyone else's agenda instead of yours. No one is going to be more interested in your Brilliant Difference than you. This is your roadmap to selling with ease, attracting ideal clients, and growing your business. This needs to be your number one priority.

Mediocrity is Fear's Way of Keeping You Safe

When you are in love with you and your Brilliant Difference, mediocrity has no chance. Selling from love becomes your default. Alex Linley author of *Average to A+*, writes about how to use your strengths and make the most of them[2]. In his book, they conducted research on a traditional assessment process in corporate environments called a "360". This is when an employee receives feedback from the manager, peers, and direct reports. The objective of the assessment is to give the employee a full view (hence, 360) on strengths, weaknesses, and opportunities to develop as a leader based on these various perspectives. Once the assessment is complete, the employee reviews the results with the leader or a coach and creates a developmental plan to close the gaps around opportunity areas. More often than not, the opportunity areas focus on the employee's weaknesses, not strengths. The employee walks away with a plan to strengthen weaknesses and, at best, manage strengths.

After a period of time, Alex and his team wanted to examine the impact of the 360 and post-assessment coaching and action planning. What they discovered was this: employees improved their capabilities in their weaknesses only slightly and strengths were maintained and, in some cases, decreased after this 360 assessment experience. What does this all mean?

Well, first, you will never get great at your weaknesses. And by focusing on your soft spots, you'll never get great at your strengths either. Many leaders spend time working on strengthening an area at which they'll never be great. They end up ping-ponging back and forth in this range of average, never really improving their weaknesses and never getting great at their strengths because they're so focused on their soft spots that they don't spend time nurturing the brilliance that naturally comes to them. This is the mediocrity trap that many get stuck in. You get stuck in delivering mediocre results, experiences, and impact.

You're not so bad that you get kicked off the team, and you're not hitting your stride in greatness because being mediocre is easy. It's easy because you don't stand out and you don't risk being judged. It's easy because expectations are lower—people expect out of you what you deliver. However, it's harder because you'll feel bored, demotivated, and unfulfilled.

You need to manage your weaknesses and you need to focus on strengthening, maximizing, and mastering your strengths. Your Brilliant Difference does not lie in your weaknesses. It lies in your strengths. You've got to come to terms with the fact that you're not going to be good, great, or perfect at everything. You've got to own what you are brilliant at and what you are dismal at. What is your Achilles' heel? That's someone else's gift. Leave them to shine at it and pay attention to where you shine.

Be aware and don't get stuck in the mediocrity trap! It is the death of your Brilliant Difference. It is where you will get sucked into selling from fear. It is the place where you haven't fully owned who you are. It's the place where you've fallen out of love with yourself.

CHAPTER TWO: FIND WORDS YOU LOVE

—

"I know nothing in the world that has as much power as a word."

Emily Dickinson

WHEN YOU COMMUNICATE you use words, tone, and body language. In a popular 1981 research study led by Professor Albert Mehrabian, it was discovered that what your listener hears when you communicate significantly depends on the tone and body language you use. Only a minimal amount of your message comes from your words.[1]

I was in Ireland and made a point of visiting the key landmark, Blarney Castle. It was the end of July and a blistering hot summer day. The main feature of Blarney Castle is the Blarney Stone. It is a limestone block of rock set atop the castle. It was placed there in 1446 A.D. To reach it you climb up a narrow, spiral cobblestone staircase, a mere 127 steps.

It has been said that if you kiss the Blarney Stone, you receive the gift of the gab. You walk away from kissing this rock with the talent of fluent, eloquent, persuasive speaking. Now, who wouldn't want that?

The line spilled out of the castle and through the castle gardens. Where I stood, the sign said it was a three-hour wait. It was hot. I didn't have a hat and there was no shade until you reached the castle. I debated if it was worth the wait and the possibility of sunstroke. When the tour bus dropped us off, our guide gave us a limited time for our visit. If I chose to kiss the Blarney Stone, my entire visit would be spent waiting in line under the burning sun and I'd miss out on seeing the castle grounds.

I chose to wait and kiss the Blarney Stone. I wasn't going to pass up the chance to walk away from Ireland with the gift of eloquence. As I waited, I marvelled that I was standing with hundreds of others waiting to kiss the stone. The power of being a good communicator was something we all wanted.

An article published by Sales Force listed the top sales skills as:

- Nonverbal communication

- Social selling

- Listening

- Negotiation

- Assertiveness (not pushy)

- Having a sales pitch

- Thinking outside the box

- Email skills

- Relationship management[2]

Whether you're emailing, negotiating, pitching, or managing your client relationships, you need to be a capable and competent communicator. With the content of what you say counting for very little of your message, where do you start?

You start with your words.

I believe that words do matter. The words you use influence what your client hears through tone and body language. When you have words you believe in, you show up with more confidence, clarity, and congruence. Your listeners pick up on that. When you have the right words, you free yourself from the worry about what you will say. You free yourself from the fear of doing it right or the need to meet a certain expectation. When you have your words, you relinquish the hold your doubt has on you. You can let go of the critical narration going on inside your head judging what you are saying and how it's landing.

When you don't have your words, it is reflected in your tone and body language. You hesitate. Your breath is short and shallow. You feel uncomfortable with silence and jump in to fill up the space. It doesn't seem to matter what you say, as long as you're saying something. You're tentative in your language, saying things like "possibly", "maybe", "perhaps", instead of using assertive, strong words like "certainly", "clearly", and "absolutely". Or your insecurities come across as overconfident, aggressive, and pushy. Nail your words and everything else takes care of itself.

Words are powerful. It's the way in which you communicate your message. Your confidence, clarity, and congruence permeate your tone and body language because you have your words. Words are not only what we say out loud, they are also what we say inside of our minds. These interior words affect how you feel and they influence your actions and behaviors. That's why they're especially important when you sell from love.

Know this: words matter. That is why I waited in line. Close to three hours later, up 127 steps, I kissed the Blarney Stone.

How to Articulate Your Brilliant Difference

You need to know the words that describe your Brilliant Difference to engage clients because having the right words will help you stay aligned and in love with who you are. Equally important, your words will help prospective clients know if you are the best fit for them.

Picture yourself at a networking event (don't break out in a sweat, we're just pretending.) Someone asks you what you do. Do you stammer, stumble to articulate a word, let alone words, that capture your Brilliant Difference? Or do you recite a complicated script you've memorized that leaves you feeling like a fake and leaves the other person backing away because they feel disconnected and confused? If this sounds familiar, know that we've all been there. We've all struggled to explain in words that we love what we offer. We've all been afraid to connect and be seen.

In my early days as a speaker, I was invited to speak at a business conference and ran into a colleague I had worked with many years earlier. I hadn't seen Sandra for years, and in my earlier days at the bank she was someone I had admired and looked up to. Sandra held a senior executive role, always spoke with ease and confidence, and she had zero arrogance about her, which always made it easy to connect with her. I don't know what came over me in that moment when our paths crossed on that conference floor. We greeted each other with a warm hug, and suddenly I time-warped back to being the young banker who needed to prove she was worthy to be in this room, with her and amongst this crowd.

I went into a long, no-moment-for-a-breath monologue, which detailed everything I was up to and had done since we had last seen each other. As soon as it was over, the silence was deafening. It was awkward and I felt awful. She stood there looking at me blankly, not knowing what to do with all that I had put down. Thankfully, she didn't need to, as the master of ceremonies invited us to take our seats as the conference was about to start. I walked away, mortified. I had just downloaded my entire resume and painstakingly she stood there witnessing and listening to the whole ordeal.

In that moment I wasn't in love with me. I lacked confidence and felt the need to be more, show more, and prove that I was worthy, because I didn't believe I was enough. I was even a speaker at this conference and yet, though I was worthy to be on that stage, I didn't feel worthy to be in my own skin.

Uncovering your Brilliant Difference and finding the exact words to articulate it gives you clarity and confidence to communicate your value. You stop hopping on the "all about me" soapbox where you overwhelm and ignore your listener. You stop pretending to be someone you're not. You no longer have the urge to prove your worth or deliver a performance because you're at peace and aligned with who you are and what you offer.

And on top of that you have the words to describe what makes you so brilliant!

When you sell from love, you take the time—which is an act of self-love and client-love—to prepare conversational, engaging words. These are your words, which feel right to you, to describe what you do and whom you serve best. Big, sophisticated, make-you-look smart words? You don't need them because you don't need to pretend to sell. When you download your resume or obfuscate behind jargon, it's simply a sign that you are selling from fear. And now you'll know what to do instead.

First, here are a few basic guidelines to follow as you're articulating your Brilliant Difference:

1. **Make it conversational:** You aren't writing a complicated script; you're prepping a few one-liners. Think of them more as tweets you can drop into your conversation versus something you're shouting from a soapbox.

2. **Stay away from jargon:** Use easy, simple, clear language that you connect to and understand. Don't get snared by fear trying to sound smart and don't hide behind jargon. The best practice I use is if you had to explain who you are, what you do, and the impact you deliver to a sixth-grade student, what words would you use?

3. **Start with your client in mind:** Don't jump right in talking about how brilliant and amazing you are. Yes, of course, you are awesome, but people don't care about you and what you do until they know how you can help them. People listen to you when they understand how your brilliance will help them solve their problems and achieve their goals. That is where you want to start this process: by thinking about your clients and customers.

Five Ways to Discover the Words to Describe your Brilliant Difference

Distraction, negativity bias, and getting stuck in mediocrity make it challenging to identify easily what your Brilliant Difference is. Outlined below are five practical ways for you to discover and recognize the true gifts you bring and the impact you have on others so you can connect and fall in love with who you are.

1. **Get another point of view:** Expanding your perspective is important when it comes to discovering your Brilliant Difference. You have one point of view, and it's yours. It's limited and tends to focus more on what's wrong with you, rather than what's right. This is why I appreciate this exercise: you get to hear about all the qualities and characteristics that others see in you, without blanketing it with your negativity bias. You're going to have to put yourself out there and ask others what they think of you. It does require a small dose of courage, but it's well worth it because the reward is a full bucket of confidence in return.

For this exercise you're going to email at least ten people. This can include family, friends, colleagues, employees, peers, past managers, current manager, clients, and your social media friends. The objective is to find out what others think makes you different, what you do best, and the impact you've had on them. You want this request to be simple and easy for them to do because they're busy, right? But they will make time for you and your special request.

Here are the three simple questions and one bonus question for those who want to share more with you about you:

- What three words would you use to describe me?

- What would you say are the top two to three things I do best?

- What would you say are the two to three things that make me different?

BONUS: Could you describe a moment or event where I played a significant role in delivering a positive impact on you or someone you know? What happened? What did I specifically do? What impact or result did it have for you?

When I do this exercise with my clients, they are blown away by the responses they receive. It expands the limited perspective they had on themselves. It also gives them words they would never have considered using to describe themselves. It reminds them of their gifts and the difference and value they bring to others.

2. **Complete personality assessments:** Next, you're going to expand your point of view even more. Your family friends, colleagues, clients, and managers are also limited in their view, because they get to see the version of you that shows up at home, work, or the coffee bar. They don't always get to see you fully because the environment you show up in is limited to its requirements.

For example, when you're at work, your professional, driven, results-oriented, type-A self shows up more often than your humorous, emotional, and sweet self which will show up at the coffee bar or pub with your friends and family. The context informs the content, the version of your Brilliant Difference that shows up. Getting a third-party, objective perspective is important to getting a full spectrum view on your Brilliant Difference. There are plenty of assessment tools out there and here are some of my favorites that I encourage you to explore.

How to Fascinate®:

This assessment teaches you not how you see yourself, but how the world sees you. It uses branding and marketing principles to identify your most fascinating qualities, and where you are most likely to influence and impress others. This tool will teach you all about your communication style and how to use it to your advantage. This assessment helped me identify the qualities that others saw as the best in me. It reminded me that I was an innovator, focused on excellence and challenging the status quo. This was also very different from what others in my workplace delivered. It identified not only what others saw as my best qualities, but also my different qualities. This tool will load you up with confidence as it mirrors back to you the qualities others want to see more of in you—so bring it!

Myers-Briggs Type Indicator (MBTI):

This assessment is helpful to identity if you're an introvert or extrovert. When it comes to keeping your Brilliant Difference radiating at its optimal shine you need to know how you get your energy. Are you an introvert who fuels up with downtime by reading a book or spending some time alone? Are you an extrovert who fuels up on big crowds and parties? To keep your Brilliant Difference primed for its best, knowing if you're an innie or outie is critical. In addition, with this assessment you learn how you process information, perceive the world around you, and make decisions.

Strengths Finder:

This assessment helps you identify your top strengths. This system includes a list of thirty-four strengths and, after you complete the assessment, you'll learn what your top five strengths are. The purpose of this tool is to help you discover what you naturally do best and to focus on developing your greatest talents.

Human Design:

This next assessment is a bit more on the alternative side. This system brings together the principles of the *I Ching*, astrology, Kabbalah, the Hindu-Brahmin chakra system, and quantum physics. This assessment is calculated using your birth date, time, and place, to reveal your genetic design. It's in essence a synthesis of ancient and modern sciences that provides you with simple and effective tools to enhance your life and reduce overwhelm, stress, and resistance.

Learning my Human Design type changed everything for me. It helped me understand that I was a Projector type. This type is designed to guide and needs to wait to be recognized and then invited. It took away the pressure of feeling I needed to push clients into a sale and instead taught me to market myself in a way where I could create an environment in which I was recognized and then invited by my clients. It gave me clarity on my Brilliant Difference and how to use it to attract clients and grow my business.

Enneagram:

The *Enneagram* is a system of personality typing that includes a set of nine distinct personality types. You are born with a dominant type. These personality types describe the patterns in how people interpret the world and manage their emotions. This assessment identifies your core beliefs about the world and the perspective from which you see the world.

This assessment is used in business where people gain insights into workplace interpersonal dynamics. It's also used by people on the spiritual path who are looking for higher states of consciousness and enlightenment. Whether you're looking for a business or spiritual solution, the Enneagram will help you increase self-awareness and identify areas for personal development.

3. **Reviews, awards, and testimonials:** If you work in a corporate environment, more than likely you get an annual performance review. Your performance review is chock full of insights on what you're doing right and the goals you've achieved—it mirrors back to you what your strengths are and how you made a difference in your work that year. Looking back at awards, recognitions, thank-you cards from managers, clients, and colleagues is also a great place to learn about the impact you've had on others. Clients are a great resource for feedback. They are usually very open in sharing the impact you've had on them and are willing to give you a recommendation in the form of a testimonial or referral when you've delivered on your promise.

Go back and survey your performance reviews, recognitions, awards, and client testimonials. Notice if there are any keywords that describe how you delivered your results, and what you did to make a difference. Look for things that are similar, or something that stands out that you don't do enough of and want to bring forth into your work more often.

These are the moments when your peers are celebrating you and your contributions. Most times we gloss over awards, thank yous, and review time. It can feel uncomfortable getting accolades and being singled out. But this is a time to delight in the hard work you achieved. We're so quick to move on to the next big goal that we forget to experience gratitude and the feeling of the win in the moment we are experiencing it. Take this time to relish it.

4. **Inspirational role models:** The next place I want you to go to involves considering the people who inspire you. Who would you most want to be like? Now, it may not be in every area of your life, but there are parts of you that you wish were more like someone you admire. I believe that who you are is reflected back to you through the qualities of others. What you see in them is what you see in yourself. For instance, some of the people whom I admire and am inspired by are:

Abraham Lincoln: for his ability to have a commitment to a higher purpose and the perseverance to be a voice to bring together a collective country to a peaceful agreement.

Marianne Williamson: for her ability to bring the words "God", "love", and "peace" into the modern political world. She shows me that love and business can co-exist.

Pema Chodron: a Tibetan nun I admire for her ability to teach others how to pass through our challenges and difficulties with love, grace, kindness, and compassion.

For instance, do you look up to Barack Obama? Are you inspired by his leadership presence and public-speaking skills? Are these skills you already own or aspire to have? Or is there a fitness or yoga instructor you admire for his or her personal outlook and self-discipline? Are these characteristics buried somewhere in your Brilliant Difference that you want to experience more of?

Now make a list of who inspires you. What is it about them that you admire? How does that quality show up for you? How do you want it to show up?

5. **Aspirational goals:** Napoleon Hill, author of *Think and Grow Rich*, wrote this empowering quote: "If you can conceive it, believe it, you can achieve it.[3]" I could not agree with him more. If there is a goal or aspiration you have, you can have it. This idea of who you could be, what you could do and have, is a seed that has been planted within you. Who you are and who you can become is encapsulated in your Brilliant Difference. All you need is to be open, curious, and willing to receive it. When selling from love, it's important to use

your Brilliant Difference and you do this by setting intentions, outlining goals of who you want to become and the impact you want to have. It won't come by accident, it's a conscious act and it's delivered with purpose. Who you aspire to be and what you aspire to do in this world is *who you are here to become.*

Your Brilliant Difference Blueprint

Your Brilliant Difference is something you "drip" into your conversation. People understand your Brilliant Difference best when they *experience* it in conversation, and you express it best when you tailor it to the person you're connecting with. Notice the difference: you aren't downloading a bunch of facts or fancy words about yourself but sharing bite-sized bits that fit the conversation you are having.

Here's a practical and simple framework to help you craft the words to describe your Brilliant Difference. The *Your Brilliant Difference Blueprint* includes three templates for you to use to craft and define the words to communicate your value with clarity and confidence. We'll go into detail for each of them in a moment, but here's a summary to start:

1. **Your Brilliant Difference Story:** This template will be the most in depth, detailed summary of your Brilliant Difference. Your Brilliant Difference Story is your value catchall. Whenever you need to provide information about yourself online or off, review your Brilliant Difference Story to pull out the most appropriate soundbites you need to share.

2. **Your Brilliant Difference Statement:** This next template is your Brilliant Difference Statement which includes a few short, concise statements that will not overwhelm or overload your client. There should be just enough words to create interest and engagement so you can leave a lasting impression.

3. **Your Brilliant Difference Signature:** This template is a short, two-word phrase that captures the essence of your Brilliant Difference. The first word encapsulates your Brilliance and the second defines

the impact you bring to others with your Difference. These words can often act as a positive mantra in moments when you might hold back or doubt yourself. Your Brilliant Difference Signature is a quick reminder of your Brilliance and why you need to bring it.

Your Brilliant Difference Blueprint is a living and breathing document. It's something that you have by your desk at all times. As you serve more clients you'll deliver more and better results, you'll need to update your Brilliant Difference Blueprint; as you expand your talents, skills, and expertise, you'll need to refresh your Brilliant Difference Story, Statement, and Signature. This is not a one-and-done activity, but something that evolves with you.

Crafting your Brilliant Difference takes time and effort and can feel daunting. To remove the overwhelm and help you move through this process with ease and flow, this is a good time to download the Sell From Love Workbook. You can download it here: www.sellfromlove/workbook. As you read on, you'll learn how to craft words you love to articulate your Brilliant Difference. The workbook is a practical guide to take you step by step through the process.

Your Brilliant Difference Story

Your Brilliant Difference Story is a comprehensive overview of your value and impact. Having all your words in one place makes it easy for you to pull the most relevant information you need to use for your social media channels, LinkedIn bio, internal HR talent profile system, client marketing materials, brochures, and speaking bio. For those moments when you're prepping for an important client meeting or presentation, your Brilliant Difference Story provides a valuable and foundational resource for you. Take five minutes before your meeting to remind yourself of the value you bring and the difference you deliver. This will give you the confidence to present your products, services, and best self. Your Brilliant Difference Story will remind you about all the goodness you bring, so you're better prepared when you're introducing yourself at a networking event, handling an objection, or trying to invite a client to work with you. Your Brilliant Difference Story is where you go to get inspired.

Here's what your Brilliant Difference Story includes:

Part 1: Your Brilliance: this includes your title with a brief description of what you do. Often titles are best understood by the people who work in your company or industry and not by your clients. It's always good to have a layperson's definition, so you can explain what you actually do.

Next, you need an inspiration point for your Brilliance. This could be an archetype, metaphor, or an image. It's taking your Brilliance and summing it up in a few words. You can find inspiration from metaphors, heroes, symbols or even personality tests you've taken. They usually have terrific archetype or profile names that you could use such as the change-agent, the advocate, the mediator, the adventurer, or the architect. These inspiration points provide you with powerful internal words. They drum up a quick image, a visceral emotion, and connect you to the essence of who you are and what you're here to do, quickly. For moments of doubt when you lose your north star, this inspiration point can be the extra nudge that gets you to stay in your lane, raise your hand, hit publish, or make the ask.

And finally, we have the summation of your brilliance. This is where you'll have a full list of one-liners capturing your expertise, talents, gifts, experience, strengths, skills, personality traits, and communication style. You don't include everything and the kitchen sink here. You include what's most important and relevant to the prospective client you're talking to. Use the feedback you received in your performance reviews, personality tests you've taken, client feedback you've received, and characteristics of aspirational role models and summarize it in your top ten brilliance value statements.

Part 2: Your Difference: Now that we've taken care of your brilliance, we can turn the lens on who it's for and the impact your Brilliant Difference makes. Identifying the specific person you're here to help is important. Just like you, your clients come with a unique and distinct profile. You need to know who they are and what they want. When selling from love, you need to know them inside and out. This means having the intel about your client's demographics and their psychographics. You want to know what their life looks like on the outside—family, career, hobbies, gender, age—but also what life looks like on the inside: their fears, dreams, feelings, and needs.

In addition to this, your client has a specific world view and core beliefs about how the world operates. These core beliefs are inherited and acquired over their lifetime based on their upbringing and their life experiences. Does your client have the attitude towards life of a cup half full or half empty? Do they believe in a competitive or cooperative world? Do they believe that hard work or luck is a determinant of success and fortune? Their core beliefs are important to uncover to better understand what motivates them and why they make the decisions they do. If you know your client's world view is that life is a cup half empty, you know your client will want to know you've considered and addressed any potential red flags on their behalf. This will make it easier to move forward with your client knowing that negative consequences have been mitigated.

Next, the most important part of your Brilliant Difference Story is the difference your client is looking to gain. This difference is the change they are seeking. Their current experience is not satisfying them, and they want something new. They need or want something that they don't have. For instance, a life coach starting a new business is struggling to find clients, build credibility, and make it easy for potential clients to learn how to best work with him or her. The difference they are seeking is something that will help them get clients and grow their business. A website designer is someone who can help them create this change. By crafting a personalized business website, this life coach will attract clients and have authority in his or her domain, while at the same time grow their business to fulfill their dream of building a lifestyle business, where the client is not tied to a desk, office, or location. This is the difference; the website designer delivers with his or her brilliance.

In chapter seven: "Love the Transformation, Not Only the Transaction", we'll do a deeper dive into the difference and transformation your client is seeking. This will give you additional insight on how to uncover the difference your client is desiring to create.

The final most important words in your Brilliant Difference Story is the impact and result you deliver. What transformation will your clients experience because of working with you? This is the promise you are committing to deliver. When describing the result your product or service delivers, it's important to describe the tangible, practical life change. You want to be clear about the change to the external life situation. Secondly, you want to be clear about the change to the internal state of being your client will feel. When illustrating the tangible change, adding a quantitative result helps—for example, the client will save $1000, will make $1000, or will save ten hours. Here are a couple of examples illustrating how to describe the difference your Brilliant Difference delivers:

Website Designer	
Client's life situation before your Brilliant Difference	Life coach starting a new business, has no clients or revenues coming in. Feeling discouraged and defeated before they have even started.
Client's life situation after your Brilliant Difference	Has a clear and concise website that makes it easy for clients to understand how to hire and buy their services. Since launching the new website, sales have increased by 35%. Feeling confident and ready to promote the business online.
Financial Adviser	
Client's life situation before your Brilliant Difference	Renting and living paycheque to paycheque. Feeling uncertain and experiencing anxiety about the future.
Client's life situation after your Brilliant Difference	Have a financial plan that helped save $50,000—enough for a down payment on a dream home. Feeling grateful and excited about the future.
Chiropractor	
Client's life situation before your Brilliant Difference	In lots of pain with difficulty getting out of bed in the morning and playing with their young kids. Feeling guilty and uneasy.
Client's life situation after your Brilliant Difference	Pain-free with an easy and early morning rise and is enjoying playing soccer with his three boys. Feeling connected and engaged.

Now that you know all of the components that go into crafting your Brilliant Difference Story, let's take a look at how it all comes together.

Your Brilliant Difference Story – example

Your Brilliance	Title	My name is Finka and I'm a Leadership Coach + Workshop Facilitator.
	Inspiration Point	I like to think of myself as a Trendsetter. Or… I like to think of myself as an Unwavering Wisdom Warrior. *Please note, this may not be what you say out loud, more of an internal anchor and inspiration.
	Top 10 Points of Brilliance	1. What this means is I'm the kind of person that sees five steps ahead. I'm a visionary who looks to the possible, always moving towards the positive and the highest potential outcomes. 2. I'm progressive and cutting edge in my thinking. My insights are deep, thoughtful, and not trans-actional, short-term, band-aid fixes, but rather breakthrough transformational solutions. 3. I'm self-propelled; other than the passion for the person or project, I don't need more motivation to take action. 4. My "secret sauce" skills are facilitating, coaching, storytelling, and writing. 5. I connect through emotion and empathy, telling true and transparent stories.

Your Brilliance	Top10 Points of Brilliance	6. I practice what I preach, always moving towards the edge of my comfort zone, learning, growing, and practicing internal confidence. This helps me be a better, humble human and resonate with the people I serve.
		7. I move to action with thorough research, filling up my knowledge bucket which provides me the support to execute. I love to learn, either diving deeper into a topic or learning something completely new.
		8. The Sell From Love framework is built on my over two decades career in sales and on a foundation of research that includes 235 global interviews with entrepreneurs, financial advisers, coaches, consultants and service-based professionals.
		9. I've worked with more than 10,000 people in online and live workshops, at conferences, from the stage, as well as in one-on-one sessions to help them craft their personal brand/Brilliant Difference value statements.
		10. I developed and delivered sales training programs and have coached/ observed more than 800 coaching conversations with leaders and their teams.

Your Difference	Client: Who do you work with?	• I work with ambitious, creative, heart-centric people. • I help service-based professionals, leaders, and entrepreneurs. • I work with people in the financial industry, professional development arena, and service-based professionals.
	Difference: What change are you helping to create? (Before they work with you)	• I help professionals who aren't getting enough clients or generating the revenue they need in their business. • Selling feels like they are pushing something on to their clients; it's inauthentic, feels out of alignment, takes a lot of effort, demoralizes, and exhausts them. • Putting themselves out there to network, market themselves and their services puts them out beyond their comfort zone. • They are filled with fear, uncertainty, and overwhelm.
	Process: What offer do you use to facilitate this change?	Your product or service go here: • Your Brilliant Difference Personal Brand Course • Your Brilliant Difference Team Building Workshop • Sell From Love Coaching Program

Your Difference	Results: What results or outcomes do you help your client get (after they work with you)?	• Built trust and stronger relationships • Increased leadership effectiveness and team effectiveness • Recognized untapped potential in employees • 38% Improvement in understanding of value and impact • 41% Increase in confidence • 38% Improvement in communication skills • 56% Improvement in ability to use their personal brand • 235% Increase in client loyalty • 163% Increase in coaching skills • 25% Increase in employee engagement • 98% of participants definitely recommend our training programs

Your Brilliant Difference Statement

Now you may be thinking, how the heck are you going to recall your entire Brilliant Difference Story when you're introducing yourself at a networking event, handling an objection, or trying to invite a client to work with you? For those moments when you need a quick snapshot of your Brilliant Difference, this is a way to capture the value you bring in a short-hand statement. This version comes in handy when you get asked the dreaded question: "What do you do?" It is concise enough for you to recall easily.

Your Brilliant Difference Statement Template

Topic	Sentence Starter	Your Brilliant Difference Highlight
Client: Who do you serve?	I help...	
Difference: What change do you help to create?	Who struggle with... or Who want...	
Result: What outcome do you help your client get?	I help them get...	
Process: What offer do you use to facilitate this change?	Using our...	
Transformation: What outcome and feeling your clients receive?	Ultimately...	

This is one for my business:

Topic	Sentence Starter	Your Brilliant Difference Highlight
Client: Who do you serve?	I help...	I help service-based professionals and business owners.
Difference: What change do you help to create?	Who struggle with... or Who want...	Who doubt their value and struggle to sell their services.
Result: What outcome do you help your client get?	I help them get...	I help them get clients and grow their business.
Process: What offer do you use to facilitate this change?	Using our...	Using our coaching and training programs they...
Transformation: What outcome and feeling your clients receive?	Ultimately...	...ultimately learn how to sell with authenticity, confidence, and integrity intact.

Here are a few more examples:

EXAMPLE 1: Financial Adviser

Topic	Sentence Starter	Your Brilliant Difference Highlight
Client: Who do you serve?	I help...	I help young professionals in their twenties, thirties, and forties.
Difference: What change you help to create?	Who struggle with... or Who want...	Who struggle with having clarity about their money and want to stop making haphazard decisions about their finances.
Result: What outcome do you help your client get?	I help them get...	I help them get on track to reach multiple financial goals simultaneously.
Process: What offer do you use to facilitate this change?	Using our...	Using our Gen Y personalized financial planning advice and action plans they...
Transformation: What outcome and feeling your clients receive?	Ultimately...	...ultimately match their values to their money so they can live an incredible life.

EXAMPLE 2: Marketing Consultant

Topic	Sentence Starter	Your Brilliant Difference Highlight
Client: Who do you serve?	I help...	I help business owners and educators.
Difference: What change you help to create?	Who struggle with... or Who want...	Who struggle with marketing their business online.
Result: What outcome do you help your client get?	I help them get...	I help them bypass overwhelm, self-doubt and take action to build a profitable business.
Process: What offer do you use to facilitate this change?	Using our...	Using our email list-building courses and online teaching strategies they...
Transformation: What outcome and feeling your clients receive?	Ultimately...	...ultimately, build an online business and life they love.

EXAMPLE 3: Dentist

Topic	Sentence Starter	Your Brilliant Difference Highlight
Client: Who do you serve?	I help...	I help patients.
Difference: What change you help to create?	Who struggle with... or Who want...	Who struggle with having confidence in their smile.
Result: What outcome do you help your client get?	I help them get...	I help them create a beautiful smile.
Process: What offer do you use to facilitate this change?	Using our...	Using our ease-of-mind treatment and state-of-the-art digital smile design technology they...
Transformation: What outcome and feeling your clients receive?	Ultimately...	...ultimately walk away with a customized smile that enhances their confidence.

Your Brilliant Difference Signature

Your Brilliant Difference Signature consists of two simple words that may not always be as easy to define. That's why I left this one to the end. It's easier to figure out your Signature once you've crafted your Story and Statement. Encapsulating your essence in two words feels limiting and restrictive. Your brain will resist as fear will try to tell you otherwise. However, if and when (I have faith in you!) you do this, you will fundamentally shift how you show up, as well as results you create. By getting this specific, this concise, and by being this clear, your Brilliant Difference will not confuse your clients, but will differentiate you from every other coach, consultant, agent, broker, dentist, wellness expert, adviser in the marketplace.

Just think about Steve Jobs and Apple: "Think Different". These are their two words. It's more than a slogan or a tagline and more than their brand, or any marketing strategy and advertising campaign. It defined who they were, their purpose; it was their north star. It defined the impact and results their customers experienced. It defined who their customers got to be because they bought their products and services. Your Brilliant Difference Signature has a trifecta value effect because it:

1. Defines your value

2. Determines your impact

3. Describes your clients' experience

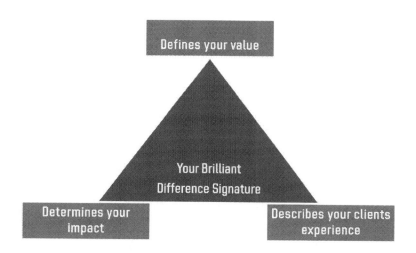

Crafting Your Two-Word Brilliant Difference Signature

1. When crafting your two words, keep in mind that you want your first word to describe your Brilliance and the second word to describe the Difference and impact you bring.

2. Be sure to review your personality tests, testimonials and feedback, inspirational role models: what themes, words, or similarities are you noticing?

3. Reflect on your Brilliant Difference Story and Statement: are your two words already somewhere in there?

4. Use a thesaurus to find substitutes for words you like, but don't love. You'll discover similar words to the word you like and, somewhere in there, find a word you love.

5. Narrow down your list to your top three contenders and ask clients, colleagues, friends, and family for feedback. Ask them to pick which one would best define and describe your Brilliant Difference.

6. Put your Brilliant Difference through the Value Triangle test. Ask yourself: Do these two words define your value? Do these two words determine your impact? Do these two words describe your clients' experience? When you get a yes to all three of these questions, you've got your Brilliant Difference Signature.

7. Use the Brilliant Difference Word Library. This is a list to help guide and inspire you to find your Brilliant Difference Signature. First, think about your Brilliance and scan the list. Circle any words that resonate with you and describe your Brilliance. Next, looking at the same list and using a different color pen or marker, scan this list and circle any word that strikes a chord with you that defines the value you bring or impact you deliver.

Using the scenarios above with our financial adviser, marketing consultant, and dentist, here a few Brilliant Difference Signature examples:

Example	Brilliant Difference Signature
Finka	Transformational Love
Financial Adviser	Intuitive Collaboration
Marketing Consultant	Radiating Lifestyle
Dentist	Elegant Confidence

Your Brilliant Difference Word Library:

When reviewing the word library, use the words as an inspiration point. Your Brilliant Difference Signature could be a derivative of the words listed. For instance, your inspiration word is 'organize', which means you could use spinoffs from that word such as organization, organizer, or organized.

Let's say you're an interior designer and you've selected two words: Organize + Style. Putting these two words together in different ways will convey a different message. For example, your Brilliant Difference Signature could be 1) Organized Style or 2) Style Organization.

For option 1, "Organized Style", you as the interior designer bring your gift of organization so that your clients will experience a sense of style and know they're up to date on the latest trends.

For option 2 "Style Organization", you as the interior designer bring your sense of trendsetting style so that your clients can have a life that is organized and gives them peace of mind.

Two words with two different meanings. Each unique, that convey two distinct Brilliant Difference Signatures.

To get clarity and confirmation on which two words best define and describe Your Brilliant Difference Signature, use the Value Triangle to ask yourself:

1. Do these two words define your value?

2. Do these two words determine your impact?

3. Do these two words describe your clients' experience?

Your Brilliant Difference Word List

authentic – elegant – loyal – style – image – beauty- service – creative – unique – individualized – graceful – intuitive – pure – refined – powerful – strong – straight-forward – compassionate – driven – ambitious – considerate– kind –strong-willed – changeable – flexible – delicate – diplomatic – fair – bold – calm – comfort – flow – genuine – confidence – friendly– serenity – brave – audacious – sassy – resolute – discerning – radiant – poised – daring – courageous – relentless – definite – dramatic – open – receptive – clear – forward – fresh – fearless – approach– results – revolutionary – integrity- feminine – masculine – connection – natural – inspire –tolerant – motivate – action – steady – spirited – ingenious – vitality – caution – care – sparkle – trust – vigor – strength – determination – structure – devotion - principled– generosity – magic– energy – insight – perspective - classy – assurance – consensus – work-ethic– empathy – harmony – collaboration – problem-solving – love – transformation – tradition – composed – tailor – personalized – fierce – cherished – independent – moral – decisive – openminded – imaginative – quick- strategic – analytical – original – thinker – enthusiastic – objective – honest – efficient – potential – charismatic – knowledge – purposeful – convincing – passionate – altruistic – idealistic – reliable – leader – curious – observant – communication– direct – responsible – respected – smooth– practical – patient – clever – organization – warm – sensitive – optimistic – spontaneous – relaxed - gallant – perceptive– rational – entrepreneurial – focus – positive – dutiful – deliberate – inclusive – adaptable – discipline – learner – intellect – significance – resourceful – balance – system– expertise – educate – design – growth – fun – facilitate –versatile– cooperation – character – coach – autonomy – proactive – quality – professionalism – nurturing – momentum – mindfulness – mentor – security – sincere – solution – standard – dependable – grit– resilience – wisdom – relatedness – precision – risk-taking – fairness – attitude – discovery – adventure – influence – planning – talent – vision – understanding – success – experiment – support – forethought – rigor – accuracy – playfulness – humor – tenacity – humble – instruction – thorough – invention – ethic – guide – model – artistic- contribution – consistency – network – management – stamina – difference – responsiveness – community – mindset– mastery – commitment – conviction – informed – impact – expressiveness – dedication – performance – venture –different – thoughtful – skillset – excellence – brainstorming.

Choosing your Brilliant Difference Signature

One of the hardest decisions you'll need to make is choosing the two words for your Brilliant Difference Signature. Whenever we're faced with making a decision or one that will limit our options, our brain will do what it does best, protect us from making a limiting and constricting choice. It fears that if you choose one, you'll miss out on something else. But this protection method will only hold you back from fully owning your true gifts and will prevent you from using them to help the clients that need you most. Remember, choosing the words to define your Brilliant Difference Signature won't be easy. Be prepared for resistance to show up.

So, how do you choose? When deciding on your Brilliant Difference Signature, you don't want your two words to describe what you already do and that which comes easily and naturally to you. Your Brilliant Difference Signature is not in your comfort zone; rather, it's on the edge of your comfort zone. Your Brilliant Difference Signature is who you are and, more importantly, it is who you are becoming. It is nudging you to grow, expand, and evolve. It should make your heart beat a little faster because you're inspired, excited, and feel exhilarated as you're entering your courage zone.

Your Brilliant Difference Signature will also grow with you. It's not a one-and-done process. Your two words are something you will review and revise, and eventually when they too become easy, comfortable and second nature, you'll know it's time to update your Brilliant Difference Signature. When you sell from love, you're always being invited to up-level your Brilliant Difference Signature.

When I started doing this work, my Signature was: Brilliant Difference. It was through owning my own brilliance that I learned to teach others how to own and use their true gifts to bring meaning and impact back into their work and lives. It was something I was and someone who I was becoming. Over time, I've become and learned fully to embody and teach others how to use their Brilliant Difference in their business and work. That has now become second nature. Today, I'm being invited to up-level my presence and impact. Today, my Brilliant Difference is Transformational Love. Sell from love is a progressive, conscious, and compassionate sales model. It's one that is transforming the current way in which we sell, market, and grow our businesses. It's also one that embodies kindness and endeavours to bring more love into the world. That is the difference and value Transformational Love delivers.

When you define your Brilliant Difference Signature, you'll walk into a room with more confidence and purpose. You'll know the value you bring, and the impact others get to benefit from it. It takes time to craft, but your effort and energy will be rewarded in spades.

How to Sell From Love Using Your Brilliant Difference

Now that you have found the words you love to describe your Brilliant Difference, here are four easy tips you can apply immediately to connect with clients:

1. **Prepare:** Finding the words to describe your Brilliant Difference doesn't come to you without work. You need to invest the time and effort to get clarity.

2. **Practice**: Being confident in communicating your Brilliant Difference only comes from practice. Read and reread your Brilliant Difference Story, Statement and Signature and try them out with friends and family. You want your words embedded into your memory so they can flow without a second thought.

3. **Prioritize:** When communicating your Brilliant Difference, lead with what's most important to your clients. Focus on the problems they are experiencing that you are ideal to solve. The outcome will be real connection with your clients.

4. **Personalize:** Pay attention to situations you're in and, depending on the audience, determine what would be most relevant to them. I was at a conference and met a financial adviser who had just entered the business a year earlier. During my conversation, even though I work with various service-based professionals, I only focused on sharing my experience working with financial advisers and my experience

in that industry. You're making it all about your prospective client, sharing what they would care most about.

When talking to prospective clients you know you've nailed your value proposition when they respond with something like: "Can you tell me more about how you do that?" Or "I know someone who sure could use that." To help your Brilliant Difference make its mark, you'll need to work with your clients, put yourself out there on social media, attend events, and reach out.

Making the time to find your words will help you fall in love with you. You walk away understanding who you are and who you're not. You give yourself permission to be you. This is not only an act of love towards yourself, it's an act of courage. You choose to model authenticity which gives colleagues and clients an inspiration point so they can choose to be more of who they are. You do you, so they can be themselves too.

CHAPTER THREE:
MOVE FROM COMFORT TO
COURAGE WITH LOVE

———

"Owning our story and loving ourselves through that process is the bravest thing that we'll ever do."

Brené Brown

SELLING REQUIRES YOU to put yourself out there and to market and promote yourself. Selling requires you to network, attend conferences, and meet new people. Selling also requires you to prospect, make calls, and ask clients to do business with you. Any one or all of these can trigger an out-of-comfort-zone moment. These moments can evoke fear and doubt which will immediately move you away from selling from love and toward selling from fear.

Here's the thing: you can still sell from love *and* be out of your comfort zone. One thing we get confused about is thinking we must feel at ease to sell. Not at all. It may not always be comfortable to sell; however, the way you love and take care of yourself can make it comforting. Self-love and self-care are how you make it safe to sell out of your comfort zone without falling prey to fear.

How well you love and take care of yourself during the selling process not only determines the success and impact you experience but, most importantly, how resilient and resourceful you become. For instance, whether you end up with a sale after a client meeting or if it didn't go as well as you wished, you can recover quickly—without falling into fear. Self-love and self-care are key strategies you need to sell from love and achieve the results you want in your business and for your clients.

Selling from love is a practice of self-love. Instead of being your own harshest critic, you learn how to be your own best friend with kind, loving self-talk, encouraging yourself as you connect with your customers and clients. You learn how to give yourself permission to act outside your comfort zone with compassion and trust. You foster a commitment to love yourself, even in moments when you aren't feeling the love. You learn to choose love, kindness, and compassion in lieu of being berated by your inner critic. Ultimately, selling from love invites us to learn how to love ourselves fully so that we are open to receive the happiness, success, and fulfillment life offers.

I recall the first program I offered online. I crafted a twelve-week marketing plan to attract ideal clients to an online personal branding course. It included blog posts, social media articles, webinars, and an email campaign. I've always been in some form of selling my entire career—however, never online. This was a first for me and completely out of my comfort zone. You see, when you send an email or post online, it goes into the ether. It's a big void. You don't know who's reading it, you're not getting feedback, nor are you making a real-life connection. This threw me into a tizzy. It was like I got amnesia.

Even though I was confident in my content and ability to connect authentically to clients, doing it online was a whole other ball game. It was awkward. It was uncomfortable. There were moments where I failed miserably. This was material I had presented in live workshops dozens of times and knew inside out, but my nerves and fear got the better of me. During the webinar

I got so nervous that I stuck to my notes and lost my personality. I recall the night before my early bird registration was about to expire. I prayed no one would sign up so I could cancel the course and pull it off my website. My prayers were answered, no one registered and with relief I took it down.

I could have spent the next weeks and months berating and punishing myself for failing miserably and quitting before I got to the finish line. Instead, through introspection and a whole lot of self-love, I reflected, reframed, and relaunched my course online.

I realized this was a first for me. I'd never sold anything online. In lieu of harsh, punitive self-talk, I was kind and self-compassionate. I reframed my situation, telling myself I didn't fail—instead I received feedback. The feedback was that online selling was new, unfamiliar, and going to be uncomfortable. I also knew there were some things I could do to create more comfort and less fear next time around.

I relaunched, using the same twelve-week marketing campaign with a tweak. Instead of selling the course directly off my website or asking for the sale in my webinar, or hoping someone in the internet ether would enrol, I invited interested clients to have a conversation first. It was through this personal, intimate, one-to-one real connection that the fear of the internet ether was transmuted. I got to connect with real people, and they got to connect with me. This time my course filled up with ease and love.

Selling from love doesn't mean you play it safe and stay in your comfort zone. On the contrary, selling from love means that you take the leap, even if fear is present, but you do it from love. With love as your guide, you can rest assured that when you leap, you'll land with two feet firmly placed in your courage zone.

Consciously Choosing to Go Outside your Comfort Zone

The best way to start overcoming your fears, uncertainties, or doubts about selling is to acknowledge they exist. Yes, of course there are times when your selling activities feel easy and comfortable. However, when you're reaching for your highest potential or looking for new opportunities, you'll need to spend more time in your courage zone. If everything you're doing feels comfortable right now, you may be hiding from your highest potential and playing small.

Ever since I was a little girl I've always wanted to teach. But my path led me to financial services instead. In all of my roles, I've had an opportunity to bring in some elements of teaching and training, but I wanted more. While holding down a full-time job I started a side hustle. I opened a coaching and training business. This was my chance to step outside my comfort zone, start a business, and eventually get in front of a room to teach full-time.

I got my first gig. It was a global, F500 company with more than 135,000 employees in the electrical energy sector. Having only ever working in financial services, the magnitude of this organization and industry were completely outside my comfort zone. I was invited to conduct a full-day team-building and communications workshop with the mechanical engineering executive team. I was way out of my league. Even thinking of it now makes my heart palpitate—what was I thinking?

Aboard my flight, en route to deliver this workshop, I feverishly reviewed my PowerPoint slides. Not only was I freaking out about my first real workshop, I was petrified of flying. This was a courage zone double whammy. Please don't try this at home.

The pilot turned on the fasten seat belt sign and announced we were going through a pocket of turbulence. As I buckled up and gripped the arm rails for dear life, the first thought that crossed my mind was "If we crash, at least I won't have to do this presentation." I was so afraid of doing this event that death seemed a reasonable option.

Getting outside your comfort zone won't always feel like this—thank goodness! You can do it gradually and purposefully, which I eventually learned, was the better way. Being aware and acknowledging that an action, task, or activity is out of your comfort zone is the first step. The next step is choosing to step outside your comfort zone so you can experience your courage zone.

The Journey from your Comfort Zone to your Courage Zone

In your comfort zone there are actions, tasks, activities, selling situations, and clients that come easily and don't make your heart beat fast or your mouth go dry. For the most part, you don't procrastinate these to-do's. You've done them so many times, you need not think twice about them.

Now your courage zone? These are often actions, tasks, and activities that feel daunting and overwhelming. You tend to put them off. They are actions you want or need to do to get more clients, serve more people, and grow your business. But fear, uncertainty, doubt, guilt, or expectations for a certain outcome hold you back. We'll do a deeper dive into these specific areas of selling from fear and how they bridle you back later in this chapter.

It might seem that it's a perfectly justifiable reason not to attend a networking event because you happen to be very busy that week and you were overwhelmed by the number of professionals there last year. You simply negotiate a rational reason why it would not be a good use of your time to attend. For that big workshop opportunity I mentioned earlier, I easily could have rationalized that I was too busy with my full-time job or that I couldn't travel because my husband and daughter needed me at home. If I had, I would not have gotten on that plane and delivered the workshop. But then I can guarantee you I would not be doing this work today. That was a courage zone moment I said yes to, even though it was uncomfortable and nerve-racking.

COURAGE
zone

Where your
highest potential
+ impact reside

your
COMFORT
zone

Your highest potential and biggest opportunities are waiting for you. They are in your courage zone and this is where the magic happens. However, as you already know, your brain's job is to keep you safe, and anything that takes you outside of your comfort zone will put your brain on alert and create resistance, as well as nudge you to sell from fear. To reach your highest results, deliver your best performance, and make the meaningful impact you want to have with your clients and in your business, you need to be where the magic happens: your courage zone.

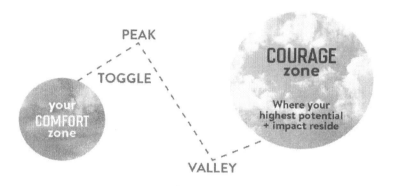

The journey to your courage zone never happens in a straight line. It's not as simple as saying you're going to get outside your comfort zone, call a client, ask them to set up a discovery meeting and bang, you get an easy yes. First, there's gathering the knowledge you need to convey why they must meet with you, there's mustering up the courage to make the call, negotiating to a yes and, if you get a no, dealing with the rejection without beating yourself up.

These are all micro courage zone moments in this macro scenario. You dip your toe into your courage zone, test out the waters and, if it's too cold—for example, you don't get a client to agree to a discovery call—you go back to your comfort zone. Just learning how to make a call that leads to a discovery meeting can go on for a few days, weeks, or even months. You toggle back and forth, learning what works and what doesn't. Success makes it easier to stay in your courage zone and setbacks may pull you back into your comfort zone. But as long as you keep showing up with self-love and self-care, you will find yourself living more of the time in your courage zone.

This process of comfort to courage never ends. Over time, you learn to perform an activity that was once in your courage zone with confidence—which moves it into your comfort zone. The ultimate benefit of moving from your comfort zone to your courage zone is building love and confidence in yourself. Every time you conquer one courage zone activity, you build more trust and faith in yourself. That's how you build confidence: the more courage zone moments you experience, the more confidence you get. Who doesn't want more confidence? When you sell from love, your aim is to up-level continually, to learn, and to unlock your highest potential. Continually looking for ways to enter your courage zone will lead you directly there.

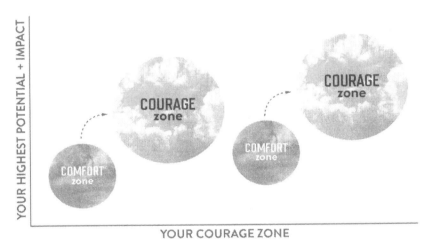

Over time, presenting workshops to small groups for clients outside my industry expertise didn't feel so scary—or put me in situations where death over public speaking was a preferred option. I learned that regardless of industry, we're all human, struggling with the same kind of stuff. Eventually I was back in my comfort zone. The next courage zone moment was speaking to larger groups, from a stage, delivering dynamic and impactful keynotes, not only workshops. Over the next few years, I continued to toggle back and forth from my comfort zone to my courage zone, from facilitating workshops to small groups to getting on stage delivering keynotes for large audiences—all while learning how to love myself even in the midst of the discomfort of fear.

Identify Your Comfort to Courage Zone

To identify what activities, actions, and clients are in your comfort and courage zones, here's a quick exercise you can do. There are two parts:

- Part 1 is identifying what activities, actions, and clients are in your comfort and courage zones.

- Part 2 is deciding what action you're going to take based on what you identified in part one.

You want to use this exercise to decide where the best use of your valuable time and energy will be spent.

Here are three landmarks in your comfort to courage zone:

1. **Comfort Zone:** An activity or task that you're already doing that is completely comfortable.

2. **The Edge:** An activity or task that takes effort and feels slightly to moderately uncomfortable.

3. **Courage Zone:** An activity or task that takes effort and feels moderately to extremely uncomfortable.

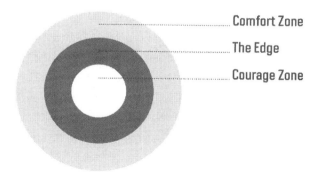

Comfort Zone
The Edge
Courage Zone

When selling from love, you won't always feel comfortable. You will feel uncertain and that doesn't have to derail you. By acknowledging where your sales tasks and activities land in your comfort to courage zone spectrum, you transmute the power fear holds on you.

Comfort to Courage Zone Examples

Here are a few examples:

Linda: Consultant and Strategist for Retailers

Comfort Zone: Develop content

The Edge: Create a sales pitch

Courage Zone: Present a sales pitch

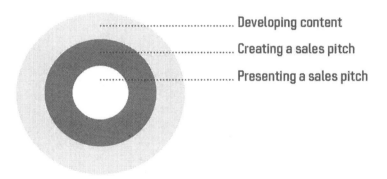

Linda is most comfortable doing research and gathering data on the challenges her retail clients are facing. It validates what she already knows about how the industry is changing with shoppers moving online rather than visiting brick and mortar stores. Her consulting program helps her clients learn how to attract more customers to their stores through experiential shopping. Preparing a sales presentation to position her ideas, expertise, and program to her clients puts her on the edge of her comfort zone. She needs to tell them why she has the perfect solution to their problem. She also has a past reference point where things didn't go so well; this resurfaces every time she needs to make a sales presentation. She begins to remember a time when she messed up in front of a client she really admired. She recalls how she stumbled over her words and felt embarrassed. She never really processed the event which has now been tattooed in her mind as a total failure.

Thinking of making the presentation pushes Linda beyond her comfort zone and into an overwhelm swirl. She doesn't get much done beyond collating the surveys, studies, and trends happening in the industry, because her real goal is overpowered by the fear she's experiencing.

Jessica: Brand and Marketing Consultant

Comfort Zone: Executing projects

The Edge: One-on-one direct sales conversations

Courage Zone: Follow-up on clients when services have been delivered

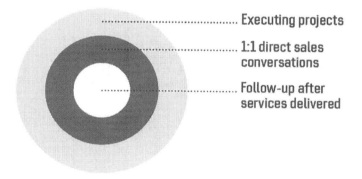

Executing projects

1:1 direct sales conversations

Follow-up after services delivered

Jessica loves to execute. She's action-oriented and likes to start and finish projects. Ticking things off the to-do list is in her comfort zone. One of Jessica's goals is to broaden her client base to increase revenues by introducing a new program. She helps her clients define their purpose and business brand. Her new service would offer her clients a way to take all their employees through an online platform where they'd learn about the company's purpose and brand. More importantly, the service would give their employees an opportunity to build their personal brands and define how they will apply it to their company's goals. Having direct sales conversations with clients about her new program puts Jessica on the edge of her comfort zone. Following up with clients and discussing next steps takes her beyond her comfort zone. Yet Jessica knows that following up is where her biggest opportunity for growth lies; follow-up conversations are the ideal time to introduce her new service. Jessica finds that the fulfillment and safety she gets from executing on projects with current clients always takes precedence over moving forward with client opportunities that will help her broaden her audience.

Kevin: Financial Adviser

Comfort Zone: One-on-one calls to people he knows

The Edge: One-on-one calls to influencers in the industry

Courage Zone: In-person meetings at conferences and live events

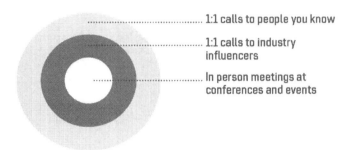

Kevin has been working with his roster of clients for two years now. Every time a new solution or service is launched by his firm, he picks up the phone with confidence to tell his current clients all about it. However, one of Kevin's goals is to grow his portfolio and develop business with real estate developers. It's a personal interest for him and he has a few contacts in the industry. He's considered reaching out to them, but hesitates, because it's on the edge of his comfort zone. There are also a couple of upcoming industry events he wants to attend, but his introverted side holds him back. Kevin feels awkward in large crowds and every time the conversation wheel turns to him, he feels flustered and has a hard time finding the right words. This activity is beyond his comfort zone.

How to Make the Leap From Your Comfort to Your Courage Zone

For Linda, naming the activities that kept her in and out of her comfort zone helped her acknowledge the fear she was feeling and how she was burying it in the inordinate amount of time she was spending on research and data collection. It helped her acknowledge that she had enough data and knew her stuff and was ready to take all that data and move to the next best step, which was on the edge: preparing her sales pitch.

For Jessica, identifying the activities in her comfort zone, such as her project to-do list, helped her see that she was holding herself back from launching her employee brand platform. This activity reminded her about her goals and priorities. It was important for Jessica to launch her new program. She held back from the temptation of project work and instead started talking to her current clients about her new program. That was the best next step for Jessica.

For Kevin, naming the activities that were in and out of his comfort zone helped him reconnect to his Brilliant Difference. He was feeling discomfort reaching out to influencers and attending conferences and events. He felt that he needed to be an extrovert, an outgoing conversationalist who could walk into any room and engage anyone in conversation smoothly. Instead he remembered to focus on his expertise and the value it brought his current clients. He also remembered that being an introvert didn't mean he was anti-social or didn't like people. Quite the contrary—he enjoyed engaging in thoughtful, deep conversations. For him it was more important to focus on building relationships than collecting business cards. For Kevin, his next best step was to reach out to influencers, not with the intent to get something from them, but to see how he could help them.

Now it's your turn. It's time to name what actions, behaviors, or clients are in and outside of your comfort zone. You can draw three circles around each one representing the various comfort to courage zone areas or visit www. sellfromlove.com/workbook to download the Sell From Love Workbook.

Leaping Headfirst into Your Courage Zone

I don't recommend that you leap from an activity that's in your comfort zone to an activity that's completely beyond your comfort zone. It can be overwhelming and creates an ideal environment for selling from fear to show up, which can sabotage your efforts. The best place to start is with an activity on the edge of your comfort zone. That way you'll build more belief in yourself and your abilities without falling back into selling from fear. The task in your courage zone will then naturally move to the edge. Working your edge is how you move more activities into your courage zone!

Courage Zone Disrupters

Making a cold call, presenting at a seminar, networking at an event, or making a proposal to a client can pull you out of your comfort zone, which means selling from fear can arise. A primary role our brain plays is to keep us safe. Any notion of fear will trigger our brains into a fight, flight, or freeze moment. The toggling back and forth when you attempt to move from your comfort to your courage zone could get you FUDGE. FUDGE stands for:

Fear

Uncertainty

Doubt

Guilt

Expectations

Any or all of these could show up and make the transition to your courage zone uncomfortable and something you will do anything to avoid. You are prevented or delayed from taking the action you need to sell and promote yourself. Just like eating too much fudge, when FUDGE is present, you'll feel icky and heavy. Every time you put yourself out there, it will feel as if you're carrying a load that weighs you down. Here's a snapshot of how FUDGE could derail you from your selling efforts:

Fear: Fear of failure, fear of rejection, fear of looking silly, even fear of success. What if you fail miserably at making your pitch? What if your client says no? What if you don't say it the right way? What if they say yes—can you handle the extra workload?

Uncertainty: I consider uncertainty the number one culprit in activating our survival brain. Uncertainty stops you from making the call, attending networking events, speaking at or hosting seminars, or sharing your point of view on social media. These are all moments where you don't know how people will respond or if you'll be successful. Choosing certainty always prevails and takes precedence over the unknown, no matter if there's an upside to taking the risk.

Doubt: We all have an inner voice that tells us you can't do it, you're not qualified, you don't know enough, you're not ready, and a million other one-liners that flash in our minds like Las Vegas neon lights. Again, this is your brain trying to keep you safe. Only it doesn't work and it makes your situation worse. When your negative inner voice takes centre stage, you don't make the call, attend the event, introduce yourself, or hand out your business card.

Guilt: You may need to attend a business event or a course to up-level your sales skills, and this may result in feeling guilty about spending time away from your family. Or you may be rocking the sales scorecard and feeling guilty because you're in the limelight surpassing your colleagues. Taking up space and shining can make you feel guilty so you deny your own success.

Expectations: If you worry about how hard the sales call will be, you won't make the call. If you're concerned that your client will say no, you won't promote yourself. Expecting a positive or negative outcome sets you up for failure and limits your success potential.

First and foremost, let's call out something here. FUDGE—even though it doesn't feel good, is uncomfortable, and generates resistance when moving from your comfort zone to your courage zone—is a normal part of our human experience. If you're human, at some point, you will eat FUDGE. If you're reading this and saying "no, not me", then I can't believe my book sold so many copies it made it into the hands of someone on planet Zoltar. All kidding aside, fear, uncertainty, doubt, guilt, and expectant emotions apply to everyone. It's part of our human DNA.

Here's an example of FUDGE in action:

John is a financial adviser looking for ways to drum up new business. He decides to host a financial planning seminar. The date has been chosen, the venue booked, and invitations sent. As the date approaches, John starts feeling uneasy about the whole idea. He begins to question his public speaking abilities. He hasn't spoken in front of a crowd in a couple of years, and recalls that the last time he did, he completely omitted a section of his presentation because of nerves. John begins to regret initiating the event. A few clients have called to decline and he's in the messy middle of preparing his presentation for the big day, and it's not coming together as easily as he had hoped. Here's John's FUDGE experience:

Fear: John is afraid the seminar won't work, and he'll fail miserably.

Uncertainty: He's uncertain people will show up.

Doubt: He's doubting his ability to deliver an effective and engaging presentation.

Guilt: He's already spent $1000 on preparations for the event and is feeling guilty because it may be a waste of time and money.

Expectations: His boss is depending on him to make this work. He's short on his target and this is supposed to be his big ticket out.

Selling from Fear Protection Strategies

We don't like to feel FUDGE. It's uncomfortable and just plain lousy. The best way to remove the blocks that FUDGE puts in the way is to reconnect immediately to selling from love. But often what happens is we move to the sell-from-fear protection strategies. We apply these protection strategies unconsciously. By using them, we think we'll remove the fear we're feeling, eliminate resistance towards a specific activity or task, or avoid the unpleasant outcomes we know selling from fear will cause.

Your intent in using these sell-from-fear protection strategies is good. You think these strategies will improve the situation, not make it worse. But even though your intentions are in the right place, momentarily making you feel better, the impact makes matters worse.

The five sell-from-fear protection strategies are pleasing, perfection, proving, punishment, and performance. You have an experience of FUDGE, and somewhere deep in your unconscious you decide that the best way to overcome and move past FUDGE is to choose one, some, or all these protection strategies. It could sound something like…

- If I please my clients, employees, team or manager, I'll feel safe and know I belong.

- If I dot all my I's and cross all my T's, the uncertainty will be removed because it's perfect and I'm perfect.

- If I prove I'm worthy to be in the boardroom, client's office, or networking event by declaring all my accolades, awards, and degrees, no one will doubt that I deserve to be there.

- If I punish myself with unkind, harsh words from my inner critic, I won't get complacent and forget something or slip up. I'll push myself to succeed.

- If I deliver my highest and best performance, I'll finally be good enough and I can rest on my laurels.

The thinking behind these protection strategies is that if you please enough, are perfect enough, prove you're worthy, punish yourself enough or perform to meet expectations, the fear, uncertainty, doubt, guilt, and expectations go away. Of course, they don't. All these choices do is add more fear to your life and the vicious cycle repeats itself until you're exhausted, burnt out, or no longer enjoying your work.

I had just come off a stellar performing year. I was a District Leader for Business Banking in one of the big five banks here in Canada. My team of business advisers had a steep climb by starting the year ranking at the bottom amongst the sixteen other teams nationally. They each brought their unique skills and expertise, focused on what mattered most to our clients, and showed up with empathy, and a desire to serve. Month by month, we climbed the ranks, ending the year as the number one district across Canada. Reflecting on that time, it was a perfect example of what selling from love looked like for my team—and what leading from love felt like for me. We had a common goal and purpose. Each team member was valued for their individual brilliance with full permission to use it. We focused on our clients and doing what was right for them. As a result, our clients rewarded us with more of their business and referrals to their networks. There was no pressure, only a desire and willingness to do good work. There was no fear, only a longing and commitment to be real, kind, and human.

As a result of this successful and high performing year I was rewarded with a promotion. I was asked to lead the largest district in the country. It was on Bay Street: Toronto's downtown financial core where the highest profiled clients banked. It had the largest portfolio of assets under management and sales target I'd ever had in my entire career. If this new district succeeded, then the entire country did well. This was a big load; I was carrying an enormous amount of pressure on my shoulders.

Working in this region also meant that my office was located directly in the executive epicentre. Not only was my direct manager within earshot, but it was completely normal for the regional senior vice-president, the national vice-president (VP) of sales, and the VP of service to visit my office to check in, which often felt more like an interrogation, to find out what my team was doing.

Experiences with the VP of sales, Ryan, left lasting scars. Ryan would show up at my office doorstep every morning by 7:30 am on his way back from his coffee run. Like a drill sergeant, he'd quiz me on the prior day's sales results. The expectation was that I'd rhyme from memory every individual's sales activities—the number of calls and meetings they had, and their sales, what products and services they sold, volume of sales, and revenue earned. I had a team of thirty; can you imagine how difficult a feat this was to accomplish—*every day*?

I was deep in fear. The environment and expectations were paralyzing. I feared I'd disappoint these leaders who expected so much of me. They saw something in me; I had potential and that's why they had asked me to lead the biggest area in the country. To manage all the fear, uncertainty, doubt, guilt, and expectant emotions going through my system, I used these protection strategies. I buckled in securely for a sell-from-fear ride.

I told myself, *you had better not let them down, get your act together, and make things happen.* I wanted to impress and gave in to the pressure to please the executives and prove to them they hadn't picked the wrong person for the job. Every morning I'd arrive at my office at 6:00 am, print off my sales reports, practice, and commit to memory each of my thirty team member's sales results from the day prior. I'd be armed and ready to meet the performance expectations for Ryan's tyrant probe.

I was deep in the weeds: selling from fear was my reality. The consequences of selling from fear not only negatively affects your performance and impact, it trickles into other parts of your life as well. Not only was the fear and pressure I was feeling not delivering the sales results I needed, it was affecting my health and well-being. I'm a dedicated runner and do my best to put good food in my body. I no longer made time for self-care—I had to be in the office practicing my sales number presentations for Ryan, right? I stopped working out and started fueling myself with five coffees a day, alongside sugar-filled muffins and candy. I gained weight and eventually developed a serious back condition. My body was sending me red flags that I was no longer aligned with selling from love. As if that wasn't enough, I was at risk of losing the most important relationship in my life—my husband. I was spending so much time at work trying to cope with all the fear I was experiencing that I was losing the love I already had.

Selling from fear is not only about sales results. It's about your life. The consequences ripple throughout every area. I've been a walking billboard for both of these experiences. When you sell from love, not only do your sales improve, so does your life.

Eventually things turned around. I focused on personal development by reading books that connected me back to love. I began filling up the inner narrative with words from Wayne Dyer's *The Power of Intention*, Marianne

Williamson's *A Return to Love,* and *Loving What Is* by Byron Katie. These authors and books were my mentors and coaches—not Ryan, the VP of sales. I went to therapy and began getting what was going on inside my head out in front of a professional to help me make sense of it all. I started journaling and meditating and put my runners back on. Collectively, this focus on self-love and self-care helped me regain my health, reconnect to my husband, and come back to selling from love. We'll talk more about how you can use self-love and self-care to overcome fear in the following chapter.

This story doesn't end with a rock-bottom-to-hero sales performance finish. Within ten months of taking on this role, the company restructured its leadership. My guess is they realized selling from fear wasn't working either. The entire executive team I reported to was disassembled. Ryan was no longer the VP of sales and was moved into a project role. He could no longer torment me and the rest of the leaders with his fear tactics.

This was another visceral experience that showed me the difference in selling from fear and selling from love. Selling from fear will move you further away from you, your clients, and what matters most. Even with their best intentions, the protection strategies of pleasing, proving, perfection, punishment, and performance only end up adding more to our already hearty FUDGE cake.

The Five Protection Strategies when You Sell from Fear

In order to fix something that's not working you need to be aware and acknowledge what isn't working. To move away from selling from fear it's important to identify which of these protection strategies you rely on most. I've found myself falling into the trap of each of these at one time or another throughout my selling career.

Protector Strategy of Pleasing: This strategy is all about making others happy so that you're liked. It's also about avoiding conflict so you don't have to make others unhappy or be the bearer of bad news. The desire to be liked is one we all share. Don't feel bad for wanting to be liked. However, it gets in the way when you think that people won't like you if you don't make them happy or do what they want. Pleasing your clients, manager, employees, or team can make you feel burdened with too much work and responsibility. Boundaries become loose or non-existent. Think of clients to whom you just can't say no or clients who call you on weekends or during dinner with your family. You want to deliver great customer service; you want to make them happy, but it's infringing on the quality of work you deliver and life you live. The temptation to please provides temporary relief but creates heavy baggage and unrealistic expectations that will weigh on you and your selling efforts.

Protector Strategy of Perfection: Perfection is a protector strategy that is influenced by the positive intention to deliver excellence and a high quality of work. You want to deliver exceptional work, ideas, and solutions to your clients. However, this protector strategy gets in the way when you hold back your work, ideas, and solutions because you don't have everything exactly right. You resist sharing your ideas or services for fear of judgment or criticism. You want to get it perfect so that you can avoid negative or even constructive feedback. Perfection fuels procrastination. Your work stalls in analysis paralysis. You're avoiding criticism, but you're also preventing your work from shining or serving others. The irony about perfection is this: we often hold back, but it's through sharing our imperfect work that our strength is demonstrated. It's a testament to your true power, because you're willing to get feedback, get it wrong, and make it better with help from others. It shows how strong you truly are because you know you can handle it no matter how imperfect it may be.

Protector Strategy of Proving: Imagine yourself at a networking event that's filled with people whom you admire or want to work with. You may be feeling a bit over your head and unworthy to be in the same room because you don't have the same level of expertise, experience, or credentials. It's your turn to introduce yourself and you move into a long monotone monologue, recounting all your experience, all your successes, and possibly even dropping a name or two. *See, I belong here*, you're telegraphing, but not in a way that others can connect to. You think you're impressing them when in fact it is turning them off because you seem fake and showy. When it's all about you, you make it difficult for your clients to see why they'd need you. Proving is fear's way of trying to help you belong, inadvertently making you someone people want to avoid.

Protector Strategy of Punishment: Punishment is when you berate yourself with negative and critical inner chatter. It's the inner voice of judgment and criticism. It's the narration of everything you should have said or done. In this strategy, you talk to yourself harshly, like a mean boss. You post an article on LinkedIn and make a typo or you forget to ask for a referral during a client meeting and the inner criticism goes crazy. You feel minimized and diminished, pulled away from your true self and away from selling from love.

Protector Strategy of Performing: How many times have you seen the sequel to a best-selling movie fail miserably at the box office? Those movies got hit with the curse of performance and this happens to you too. You come off a phenomenal sales year, with a big bonus, awards, client success stories and accolades. Then the year starts again, right back at zero. What you did last year no longer counts and, on top of that, you have a new standard of success to hit. Not only do you have to hit your goals, you need to land in the top 10%. When selling from fear, you worry that you won't live up to last year's performance, hit this year's targets, or meet and exceed expectations you have of yourself or that others have of you. You put pressure on yourself—pressure to perform as you did the year prior. The protector strategy of performance wants you to believe that if you focus on what and how you performed last year, you could once again repeat a stellar year. By focusing on the performance that once was, it unfortunately limits the potential of what could be now, in this upcoming year. You're too busy attempting to orchestrate the same magic you once had that you lose any magic in what is present and could be now.

Let's contrast all this with selling from love. Selling from love trains you to be kind, empathetic, compassionate, and generous towards yourself and your clients. Selling from love stops these protection strategies from overwhelming you. Selling from love doesn't make you feel less than or unworthy. You don't need to compromise your integrity to sell. Selling from love is how you reconnect with who you really are, bring your Brilliant Difference, and claim your worthiness. And when you do something uncomfortable, such as asking a client to work with you, you do it in the name of love.

The Unintentional Impact When Selling From Fear

The protector strategies aren't the only result when you sell from fear. Selling from fear doesn't feel good to you and it doesn't make a good impression on others. A 2009 article published by Harvard Business Review explains that when we find ourselves in a stressful situation, lacking confidence or feeling the pressure to sell, we'll overcompensate, overdo, and overplay our strengths[1]. It dims the light on your Brilliant Difference.

Recall Linda, the consultant and strategist for retailers. Linda's comfort zone was doing research and developing content. On the edge of her comfort zone was taking that research to create a sales pitch and her courage zone included presenting her pitch to her clients. She experienced self-doubt and was afraid of failure. To help mitigate her fear and doubt, she initiated the protector strategy of perfection. By focusing on getting all the details just right, Linda attempted to manage the fear and doubt she was feeling. Her goal was to find the perfect research to craft the perfect pitch so she could deliver a perfect presentation.

Linda's Brilliant Difference is her ability to analyze a situation carefully before moving to action. She's an observant, active listener, and she has a knack for discerning only the most relevant details for her clients. She is thoughtful in her approach and takes pause before making a decision.

In lieu of using her Brilliant Difference to present her findings to her client with a proposed plan and solution, Linda got stuck in over-analyzing. Her fear and doubt triggered her need for perfectionism. That perfectionism spurred her to double down on her Brilliant Difference of thoughtful analysis and discernment. She was caught in analysis paralysis, unable to make a decision to move forward to present her pitch presentation. She was afraid she didn't have enough of the perfect details and this fear held her back from presenting anything.

This is how selling from fear turns your Brilliant Difference into a liability. Fear, uncertainty, doubt, guilt, and expectant emotions initiate the protector strategies. These strategies take what you do so brilliantly and double down on it, leaving the impression you least desire. What happens in these situations is we think, *Things aren't going so well, If I only bring more of X (insert your Brilliant Difference), it will make things all better and make this fear go away.* Obviously, we're not doing this consciously; it's happening without our awareness. But it *is* happening, and we must acknowledge selling from fear, so we can move to selling from love.

Let's say your Brilliant Difference is bringing confident leadership and an action-oriented approach to your clients. You help them make decisions and take forward-moving action. But when you sell from fear, your natural, level-headed, confident leadership morphs into a more aggressive, bossy, and overbearing style. Somewhere in your subconscious, you got the idea that if you brought more confidence and more force to your clients, it would improve the situation or, at the very least, make the discomfort go away. In the end it doesn't remove the fear, nor help you get any closer to making a good impression.

Here's a sample list of characteristics that may be included in your Brilliant Difference with a corresponding consequence when selling from fear turns your asset into a liability. Look and see which ones show up for you most often.

Your Brilliant Difference Characteristic(s)	Your Brilliant Difference Overcompensated
Confident, leader, decisive, action- oriented, forward movement	Aggressive, bossy, overbearing
Emotionally connected, intuitive, sensitive, empathetic, warm	Hypersensitive, irrational, impulsive
Detail-oriented, logical, rational, observant, discerning, diligent	Fussy, meticulous, uptight
Creative, out-of-the-box, innovative, forward-thinking, changemaker	Overwhelmed, chaotic, flighty
Consistent, stable, dependable, realistic, steady	Controlling, stern, inflexible

Consider your Brilliant Difference: which of the listed characteristics do you overcompensate for most often? Do you double down on the details, or bring more ideas or become more directive and bossy? Noticing where you're overcompensating on your Brilliant Difference is important so you can work backwards to reflect and identify the factors that led you there in the first place. Doubling down on your Brilliant Difference is the effect of when you sell from fear. You need to learn what caused it to change and avoid the negative impact it leaves on others. When you identify what influenced and triggered a sell-from-fear moment, you can then use self-care and self-love practices to bring you back to selling from love.

Think about which situations, environments, or people set you off. For instance, you spend too much time on social media and get hit with the comparisitis bug. Do you tell yourself you're not doing enough, or you're not doing it as well as your peers and competitors? How about when you're presenting to an unfamiliar audience or in a high-stakes meeting with affluent, highly educated executives? There's either a lot of unknowns or a lot riding on your project or presentation.

Next, think about specific triggers. For instance, you've recently had an unexpected roof repair, or your partner has been laid off and your emergency money cushion has been used up. Does the financial pressure trigger fear, which then incites the protection strategy of performance, with a result of turning your intuitive and emotionally expressive approach into being overly sensitive, dramatic, and irrational? Or did a new product or service you were excited to share with clients not sell as well as you thought it would? Did the lack of enthusiasm from your clients trigger doubt, which then incited punishment from your inner critic, and did overcompensation from your creative thinking compel you to drop this offer and go off to create a new one?

When you're aware that selling from fear has entered the arena and you acknowledge that performing, pleasing, perfection, proving, or punishment are triggering you to overcompensate on your Brilliant Difference, you can consciously choose to sell from love. Selling from love will help you navigate through the waters of fear. Self-love is your map to return back home and self-care is your compass for staying the course.

Now that you know the consequences that can arise when you sell from fear, let's take a deeper dive into how self-love and self-care can help you reconnect to selling from love. We'll take a look at specific strategies that will help you get there.

CHAPTER FOUR:
USE SELF-LOVE TO CREATE
COMFORT IN YOUR COURAGE ZONE

—

"how you love yourself is
how you teach others
to love you"

Rupi Kaur

WHETHER IT'S TIME to ask an important client to work with you, transition from word-of-mouth marketing to promoting yourself on social media, or turning your ideas and thought-leadership into a book, selling from love is how you expand your impact. That's good news because you will always have the support you need to thrive. And it's vital you recognize that selling from love often requires you to move into your courage zone where there's always a chance for fear to show up. However, self-love is a fantastic way to stop the fear, uncertainty, doubt, guilt, and expectations you experience from derailing you.

Self-love might seem as though it has nothing to do with your success, but it totally does. When you sell from fear, there is often an underlying belief or presupposition that you're not enough, that something about you or the way you are selling is inadequate or undeserving, that if you could just sell more like _____ (insert your mentor or your biggest competitor or Don Draper on *Mad Men* here) you'd be successful. You start to believe your self-talk, often without realizing it, and before you know it you're selling from fear again.

It's through self-love that you find the courage, compassion, and capability to do the things you most want to do, even though they're uncomfortable and not easy to do. Self-love helps propel you forward into your courage zone. With self-love, the world feels safe. You are stronger, grounded, and connected. Selling from love means that you love yourself no matter what.

It means that....

Even if you don't feel like you're enough, you love yourself.

Even if you don't have the credentials, experience or expertise (yet), you love yourself.

Even if you ask for your client's business and they say no, you love yourself.

Your worth and the love you hold for yourself is never determined by your sales. Even if you don't make the sale, you love yourself just the same. Self-love is how you navigate back from selling from fear and how you remain aligned and connected to sell from love. Self-love reconnects you to the love within yourself and helps you pick yourself up from failures or mistakes with compassion and kindness. You allow yourself to love yourself so much that no matter what happens, you know you'll be okay and can handle it because of the love, care, and compassion you hold for yourself.

Back in Chapter 3, I shared a story about selling my first online course. There's an addendum to the story I want to share with you here, since we're on the topic of self-love. At the time, I had hired a business coach to help me take my business to the next level. Working with Nora, my goal was to create a body of work, in the form of a book, that would serve as the foundation I'd build my business around. Nora was a writer herself, with a few published books in her repertoire and a Brilliant Difference that included marketing courses online. She directed me in a different direction. In a few short weeks, my goal of writing a book switched gears to moving full speed ahead in creating a course and marketing it online. Yes, that online course that I was praying no one would sign up for.

My original goals for the work I was yearning to do, and had hired Nora to help me with, were shelved. I questioned my goals, thought they were too big and lofty. Who was I to write a book? I should let go of these far-fetched dreams and instead follow what the expert was telling me to do. I had a bad case of imposter syndrome, and Nora wasn't encouraging me to follow my dream either; that must have meant she didn't believe in me either.

In that moment I didn't feel worthy enough to have a book to my name. I didn't have the courage to follow the deep inner voice I was being nudged to listen to. Instead of self-love, I was deep in the fog of self-doubt. It pushed me away from love and towards fear. I second-guessed myself and allowed my fear and lack of self-love to steer me away from my real goals. Following your intuition and the guidance of your inner wisdom is a demonstration of love, even in the midst of fear.

This is what Steven Pressfield, author of *The War of Art*, has to say about self-doubt:

"Self-doubt can be an ally. This is because it serves as an indicator of aspiration. It reflects love, love of something we dream of doing, and desire, desire to do it. If you find yourself asking yourself (or your friends), 'Am I really a writer? Am I really an artist?' chances are you are. The counterfeit innovator is wildly self-confident. The real one is scared to death."

I was scared to death and I needed even a mere gram of self-love to get back to what I really wanted to do: write this darn book. Even though my plans had changed while working with Nora, eventually I realized through self-love that I was still on plan. Instead of hating on myself for letting someone else direct my goals and business, I loved on myself with self-compassion and kindness. I said things like "of course you followed her advice, she's an expert; of course you put your goal of writing a book on the back burner, it's a monumental project; of course you could see all of this and choose differently today." It was through the power of these gentle words that I exercised self-love.

Looking back now, it all worked out perfectly. This body of work has more depth and is richer because of it. The entire experience of selling my first course online gave me more evidence of what it was like to sell from fear, and the practice for how to return to sell from love. I have more proof and a deeper understanding that selling from love was not a soft and squishy sales model, but instead a wise and strong one. I needed this experience with Nora to pull me off my path, away from self-love, to see that. I needed once again to sell from fear, to remember what it was like to sell from love. This was yet another moment where I needed to fall in love once again.

The Voices in Our Head

Loving ourselves is hard at times. There's the auto inner critic ready to pounce on any misstep or mishap you experience. Selling from love calls you forward to bring your Brilliant Difference and to use it in your work so you can have the meaningful impact you're here to make. Selling from love invites you to trust your Brilliant Difference by practicing replacing the voice of your inner critic with the voice of your inner champion. This is the voice that gently guides, encourages, and helps you to recover when things don't go the way you want.

Stop Listening to Yourself and Start Talking to Yourself

When my daughter was six, I took her to our community pool to teach her how to swim. As she stood by the edge of the pool, I called for her to jump in the water as I held out my arms prepared to catch her in the shallow end. Terrified to make the leap, she cried out "Mommy, Mommy, I can't do it. Mommy, I'm scared!" With a calm and encouraging voice I replied, "Yes you can. Mommy's right here, ready to catch you. Just jump!" She continued with her "I can't" and "I'm scared" cries and then something happened. She changed her words. She started telling herself:

"Jelena, you can do it. Jelena, you can do it. Jelena, you can do it!"

And with that third declaration, she jumped right in. Her face beaming with joy and excitement as the words couldn't come out fast enough, she screamed "Can I do that again?!"

This story is a perfect illustration of how the words we say to ourselves inform and influence how we show up. My daughter couldn't do the jump and was too scared, because those were the words she was listening to from the voice inside her head. It wasn't until she started talking to herself, using different words and telling herself she could do it, that she finally made the leap.

That voice inside your head is your inner critic, fueled by fear, and will cripple you and take up space unless you tell it otherwise. Like my daughter, you'll need to take the leap to ask a client to work with you, make a cold call, attend a networking event, or host a seminar to market your services. Your inner critic will tell you you're not ready, you can't do it, you don't have enough experience, you don't have a specific certification, you're too young, you're too old, you're too loud, or you're too quiet. The list goes on and on with all the reasons you can't.

Your inner critic has one objective—to keep you safe. It fears the leap: what if you make the jump to ask a client to work with you or host a seminar? Your inner critic doesn't know what will happen and fears the worst or the dreaded no. Therefore, it does its job by filling you up with reasons why you're not ready to make the leap.

Selling from love doesn't guarantee a closed sale, an easy yes, or a standing-ovation presentation. What it does guarantee is that you're empowered, and your selling comes from a place of authenticity, empathy, and integrity. What it does guarantee is you'll feel in alignment with who you truly are and your Brilliant Difference. What it does promise is you will be free to learn from your experience. And finally, it vows that the voice in your head will be that of your inner champion, speaking supportive, encouraging, kind, and loving words to you.

Your inner champion primes you with courage for the leaps and daring moments when you must get outside of your comfort zone. Your inner champion supports you with compassion through those failures when you fall flat on your face. Both voices exist: your inner critic and your inner champion. Just like my daughter by the poolside ready to make her leap, the inner critic will easily take the starting position. However, now you're aware, you can invite your inner champion to take the lead instead. Stop listening to your inner critic and get your inner champion to do the talking.

Be Your Own Best Friend

The voice of your inner critic is loud and forceful, which makes it challenging to tone down. One of the best ways to access and invite your inner champion to the table is to start from a different perspective. Let's say you have a best friend, Sarah, who has just arrived from a failed sales call. She calls you up and tells you how horribly it went. She was nervous and the client had many questions she didn't have answers to, and he didn't sign up for the service she was offering. She was disappointed in not getting the sale, but even more disappointed in herself for not knowing all the details she was presenting to him, even though it was only three months ago that she started this role.

Now, as her best friend, would you tell her she's got every right to be disappointed in herself, that she's to blame for not getting the sale, that she'll never make it and who does she think she is for even pretending she can? Of course not. But how often do you find yourself speaking to yourself this way? This mean, angry bully—your inner critic—needs to stop. It's not serving you, your clients, or the work you're here to do. It limits you.

Now, picture yourself speaking to yourself as you would to your best friend. You can already feel the difference, right? This is how you access your inner champion. You put yourself in a position as if you were speaking to a dear, loving friend. Instead of the harsh, critical words, you say something like "You should be so proud of yourself for trying; you're still so new and you took a chance to make this presentation to your client. This is all part of the learning curve and you're on the fast track because you're putting yourself out there, even if you don't know everything or have your script down perfectly. And your client is so lucky to have you: even with you not knowing all the details, you didn't want to hold back a service that you know they needed and would help them. You really should be proud of yourself."

Doesn't that sound different? Imagine what your next step would be when you speak to yourself in this tone. Instead of hiding behind your desk, procrastinating or dreading your next call, you're looking up the information you didn't know and calling your client back to let them know all about it. Stepping into your best-friend perspective will help you immediately move from the disempowering voice of fear of your inner critic and step into the voice of love from your inner champion, which will empower you to act with courage, strength, and kindness.

Positive Power Priming Your Self-talk

Establishing a new form of self-talk is important in your leadership journey to sell from love. How you talk to yourself will be a contributing factor in whether you show up to sell from love or to sell from fear. Selling is stressful and triggers many fear-based emotions. Attending a networking event where you don't know anyone or calling a potential client when you struggle with small talk: these are opportunities that make way for critical self-talk to show up. One of the most essential ways to help you sell from love is improving the dialogue between your ears. You're not a light switch: it's not easy to flip the switch to the positive, encouraging words of your inner champion. Fear and your inner critic can be deeply entrenched. But you can practice being your own champion. Over time, this practice becomes a habit.

One of the best ways to do this is through positive power-priming statements. This is a practice that will help you move from selling from fear to selling from love, especially in those comfort to courage moments. They're a tool that exchanges the habitual words of your debilitating inner critic for the strengthening and reassuring words of your inner champion, so you can initiate your actions and behaviors from love.

This practice is inspired from a technique in psychology formulated by Tulving, Schacter, & Stark in their ground-breaking 1982 study, *"Journal of Experimental Psychology: Learning, Memory and Cognition."* This theory, called conceptual priming, is now used in behavioral economics.[1]

Conceptual priming uses words to activate associated memories, attitudes, and feelings. Conceptual priming is a process that aims to influence a performance on a subsequent task. In other words, these positive power-primer statements will prepare you to get in the right mindset to sell from love. These affirming statements are a simple tool to help you take control of and direct your self-talk so it positively influences your future actions and behaviors.

Positive power-primer statements are aimed at changing the habits that get in the way of your selling from love. Power primers take the impulse you feel in your heart, the nudge that wants you to say yes to speak on stage, take your thought leadership onto social media, or proactively reach out to that influential dream client. These nudges often feel scary and make your palms sweat, but this power-primer practice offers you a practical way to bring those nudges to fruition.

The objective for these positive power-priming statements is to prime your mindset towards love and set you up for the ideal outcome you're intending to create. There are four sentence starters that go alongside each of your desired goals, needs, or feelings. Here are the positive power-primer statement starters:

I am **willing** to <insert goal, need or feeling>.

I **choose** to <insert goal, need or feeling>.

I **believe** I can <insert goal, need or feeling>.

I **am** <insert goal, need or feeling>.

These statement starters are progressive. They move you from one state of being to another in a sequence that limits the chance for fear to trip you up. They progress in commitment and confidence. You may not *believe* you can have a professional, articulate, and effortless conversation with a potential client you're about to call, but you can be *willing* to have one. Willingness is where you start. You tell yourself you're willing to have professional, articulate, and effortless conversation. Willingness then primes you to choose to have one. Making that empowering choice reminds you of a time when you felt on edge and nervous about a past client experience. That one ended well and you recall how the client couldn't wait to sign up to work with you. It happened once before and now you believe it can happen again with this new client you're currently reaching out to. Tapping into this belief stirs up a visceral memory that connects you in this present moment to the feeling of what it is like to say: I am having a professional, articulate, and effortless conversation. As you say this positive power-priming statement you tap into your feelings of confidence, certainty, and assurance right before you make your call. You have just primed your mind, your heart, and your body, using the voice of your inner champion, towards a positive outcome that you and your client will benefit from. You are now prepared and ready to sell from love.

When crafting your positive power-priming statements here are a few questions to ask yourself:

- What do you most want? How do you want to feel?

- What do you need to create the outcome you desire?

- What would success look like? What would success feel like?

Begin by responding to these questions, then take these responses to complete your positive power- primer statement starters with them. Here's an example:

Nancy, a financial adviser, is preparing to meet with prospective clients. She's done great work for one of her existing clients, who has strongly recommended her to his friends. Nancy doesn't know a whole lot about them, other than one runs a very successful business and the other is a senior executive. They both have a lot of wealth and are looking for a new financial adviser. These are dream clients for Nancy. She wants to impress these prospective clients and doesn't want to disappoint the client who gave her a raving recommendation. She's feeling nervous and she's feeling a lot of pressure to perform. She also has a seed of doubt planted: what if she can't live up to the expectations her current client painted of her to these prospective clients? She's feeling anxious and worried about her meeting. Nancy is in fear, feeling the pressure to perform and prove herself worthy of this referral; she is at risk of moving from selling from love to selling from fear.

Her inner critic begins, "You're not ready, you should cancel, they won't choose you anyways, it'd be a waste of time." She catches herself and the negative narrative running rampant in her mind. She takes a breath and notices a note she'd written to herself from the Sell from Love course she attended the month prior. She stops and remembers. There's another voice she can invite in.

She pauses and asks herself: "What do you most want to happen in this meeting? How do you want to feel? What would success look like? What would success be like for your client?"

The thing she most wants is a comfortable and confident meeting with her clients. She wants to listen, understand, and hear what they most want and are looking for. She wants to feel helpful, kind, and caring. Success isn't a sale; rather, success is helping the clients have a plan or, at the very least, options for best next steps.

Nancy has eclipsed fear and she's tapped into the power of selling from love. Selling from fear was narrowing her focus and channelling her attention only to herself and what her clients would think of her. It was focused more on preserving her identity than on serving her clients with her Brilliant Difference.

Nancy then starts with her positive, encouraging, love-based narrative from her inner champion, using her positive power-priming statements:

- I am <u>willing</u> to have a comfortable and confident meeting.

- I <u>choose</u> to have a comfortable and confident meeting.

- I <u>believe</u> I can have a comfortable and confident meeting.

- I <u>am</u> having a comfortable and confident meeting.

- I am <u>willing</u> to listen, understand, and hear what my clients most want.

- I <u>choose</u> to listen, understand, and hear what my clients most want.

- I <u>believe</u> I can listen, understand, and hear what my clients most want.

- I <u>am</u> listening, understanding, and hearing what my clients most want.

- I am <u>willing</u> to feel helpful, kind, and caring.

- I <u>choose</u> to feel helpful, kind, and caring.

- I <u>believe</u> I can feel helpful, kind, and caring.

- I <u>am</u> helpful, kind, and caring.

- I am <u>willing</u> to help my clients craft a plan and options for best next steps.

- I <u>choose</u> to help my clients craft a plan and options for best next steps.

- I <u>believe</u> I can help my clients craft a plan and options for best next steps.

- I <u>am</u> helping my clients craft a plan and options for best next steps.

She repeats these positive power-primer statements several times throughout the day and in the days leading up to her client meeting. Nancy is replacing the habitual self-talk of her inner critic and proactively injecting positive, loving self-talk from her inner champion. The negative self-talk of her inner critic has subsided. This critical self-talk may never completely go away, and this is completely normal. What you're looking for is that your inner champion is the louder voice sitting in the driver's seat, while your inner critic takes the back seat. For Nancy, her inner champion has taken the stage and has more space in her mind than the voice of her inner critic. She walks into her meeting, feeling at ease, comfortable, and confident of having a successful exploratory meeting with her prospective clients. This is a simple process to help you find the loving, supportive, inner championing voice within you, so that the inner critic doesn't flood you with fear.

This is not a one-and-done process; it's a practice that you take on proactively for those moments when you know fear is at your doorstep, ready to move you away from love. Next time you notice fear arising and those protector strategies kicking in, use your positive power-primer practice to help return back to selling from love. It's also a practice you can use proactively when moving from your comfort zone to your courage zone. The practice will prime you to an outcome that is love-based rather than fear-based. Repeat your power primers several times throughout your day: first thing in the morning and right before you doze off are important times. As you repeat your positive, love-based power primers you'll notice the voice of your inner critic subsiding. You'll steer away from fear as you connect to your inner champion and an ideal outcome that will serve both you and your client. For more resources on how to craft your own positive power-primer statements, download the Sell From Love Workbook here: www.sellfromlove/workbook.

Radical Confidence: Confidence Comes From Loving Yourself No Matter What

I was working with a financial services organization whose account managers were struggling with selling. They had built strong, loyal client relationships; however, when it came to asking for their business, their account managers hesitated, procrastinated, and avoided asking. I was invited to create a training program to help them overcome this challenge. I conducted more than seventy interviews with sales leaders and sales performers. The two questions I asked were

1. What stands in the way of your asking for the business?

2. When you do ask, what enables you to make the ask?

Hands down, the number one answer when it came to what was holding them back from making the ask was *confidence*. In order to ask for the business, they needed to have:

- Confidence in themselves and their ability to sell.

- Confidence that their client would say yes.

- Confidence that if their client said no they could recover.

- Confidence in their processes, systems, and team.

- Confidence that they, or their team, could deliver on their client promises.

Notice what was at the top of the list: *confidence in themselves*. If they lacked this personal confidence they wouldn't ask, and if they did ask they feared they'd come across like an awkward duck and would be less likely to be successful.

The dictionary defines confidence as "the feeling or belief that one can rely on someone or something; a belief in one's own abilities; having a firm trust." [2] It stems from the Latin word *confidere*, to have full trust. For many, having full trust and this feeling of or belief in confidence comes from being competent. When you have the right knowledge, skills, and experience, you feel confident. However, relying on competence to fuel your confidence is short-lived and creates an environment for selling from fear to emerge, because you'll never have all the knowledge, skills, and abilities to conquer every task or activity you'll be faced with. You'll always have room to learn and grow your expertise and craft. You're constantly going to be challenged and pulled outside your comfort zone.

And what if you've taken on a new job or role or business? Deriving your confidence from your competence can feel far-fetched. Or what if you've been given a super stretch sales target? You may struggle to believe you can achieve it. What if you're trying a new marketing strategy—let's say using social media to promote your brand? You aren't going to feel competent overnight, but you still need confidence.

Let's redefine confidence to include self-compassion, creativity, and curiosity. We might call this unconditional confidence—or at least, less conditioned. What would unconditional confidence look like? What would it feel like? It looks as though you are going into your courage zone more often and using your Brilliant Difference to serve your clients. And it means loving yourself no matter what.

Unconditional confidence invites you to be okay with the fact that you won't always know, but you're curious, creative, and resourceful enough to figure it out. Unconditional confidence invites you to be okay that you won't always feel confident, but you offer yourself compassion, gentleness, and kindness, and you'll love yourself anyway. Unconditional confidence doesn't mean that you'll close every client, but that won't hold you back from trying, because you're doing it from compassion, creativity, and curiosity.

Whenever you slip back into self-doubt or start judging yourself, use this affirmation to reconnect yourself to love:

I am confident in my ability to be curious, creative, and resourceful. Even if I don't know what to do, I do know that I am confident in my ability to figure it out.

Prioritizing Self-care So You Can Sell From Love

Self-care refuels your energy reserves, helps you stay connected to your Brilliant Difference, and diffuses the stresses you experience when selling. Ensuring you have strong self-care practices in place will help you get outside your comfort zone, outwit fear, avoid overcompensating with your Brilliant Difference and, of course, help you stay aligned with selling from love.

You can look at self-care as a mitigation strategy for when you find yourself selling from fear, or as a prevention strategy to avoid selling from fear altogether. When you don't practice self-care, it impacts how you process the events of your day, how you show up in your relationships, with your clients and the impact you have. What I know for sure is that when we don't practice self-care, we don't show up as our best and we give selling from fear fuel to take over our business.

I declared 2018 the "Year of Yes." It was my theme and I would say yes to everything. Whatever client or opportunity presented itself, no matter how big or how outside my comfort zone it was, I'd say yes. The Year of Yes proved to be a huge success. I made a strong intention to get outside my comfort zone and began putting myself out in the marketplace by vlogging regularly, being present on social media, making offers, and presenting my Brilliant Difference to clients. These actions helped me generate thirty-eight speaking events that year, numerous private coaching clients, and three sold out on-line training programs. It was one of my best years in sales and impact. But there was one flaw: I stopped saying yes to myself.

I had finished my summer speaking circuit, signed up three new private clients, and was looking forward to a jam-packed fall schedule. On the agenda was marketing and selling two more online courses, plus preparing for sixteen live workshops and keynotes. I had said yes so much that in a single day in San Francisco I had two events: in the morning I was delivering a keynote at a financial adviser conference and then in the afternoon I had another, completely separate event, a team-building workshop for an e-commerce company.

I had learned previously how important self-care was in my life. Over the years, I had started journaling and exercising regularly. I was even committed to a daily thirty-minute practice of meditation. All of this had helped me manage my energy and time beautifully but, in the Year of Yes, I became more interested in growing my business and less interested in investing time in self-care. In saying yes to every business opportunity, I had gotten into the habit of saying no to myself.

During this Year of Yes, I started to say no to self-care. Mornings would consist of internal debates about why I didn't have time to journal, exercise, or meditate. I would rationalize why I needed to tend to my inbox or put the finishing touches on a presentation and would make promises to take care of myself later. But later never came.

Stopping self-care impacted how I loved myself. I became overworked and overstressed. Even though I had the best intentions to sell from love, fear became too powerful in my overworked state. I became afraid that if I didn't say yes to a client or a speaking gig my sales would dry up. Fear of missing out, not having enough money, or saying no to a future possibility overrode my initial intention behind my Year of Yes.

For many busy professionals, self-care is the last item on our priority list—or it doesn't even make the list. When you love yourself, you make time for self-care, *no matter what*. You make yourself a priority. Taking time for self-care is a way to show love. Self-care is a practice that teaches you how to manage your time and energy proactively.

When selling, you experience various negative emotions such as fear, uncertainty, and doubt. We tend to push down these negative emotions because they don't feel good. Self-care gives you a place to process these emotions so that they don't get lodged in your mind, heart, and body. Spending a moment to contemplate and meditate, talking to a friend, or hitting the trails for a good run, are all ways that keep your emotions moving. These self-care practices help you move away from selling from fear and help you stay in alignment with your Brilliant Difference. In my case, my lack of self-care practices meant I had no way to process the nervous jitters I'd feel before I'd step on stage or moments of doubt I felt when I was selling my online course. This nervousness and uncertainty would build into anxiety and this led me to selling from fear.

There's an unexpected effect that happens when you prioritize self-care. Often, we tell ourselves we don't have time to meditate, work out, or take a yoga class. But when you do make the time, you've given yourself a time and place to process your thoughts. As you walk or run you can process your emotions about how nervous and stressed you are, and about the call you need to make. You then become more present in your day-to-day activities and tasks. Being present in turn makes you more effective, efficient, and productive. Making time for self-care is also a time-management strategy. There's a Zen proverb that goes something like this: "If you don't have time to meditate for ten minutes every day, you should mediate for an hour." An absolute sign that you need self-care in your life is when you tell yourself you don't have time for it.

If I made self-care non-negotiable, if I had made sure I was saying yes to me too, I wouldn't have ended the year in complete burn out. After thirty-two presentations I still had six to go. I spent the last five weeks of the year on the road travelling across Canada delivering a sales training workshop to financial service professionals. It was December 10. I arrived home from my last presentation, looking forward to taking the month off to spend with my family for the holiday season. But my body had a different plan. It was as if I was going 210 miles per hour and bang, I hit a brick wall. Everything stopped and my body and mind, which had been continuously on the go, didn't know what to do with itself. My adrenal system had had enough. I completely shut down. I was exhausted and my health was compromised.

I couldn't take another client, speak at another event, post another vlog, or go anywhere near social media for the next three months. I took this time, once again, to love myself and do a whole lot of self-care. I even took myself on a vacation, alone, to Sedona, Arizona for a week. I finally got the message; I knew this was going to be the last time I needed to learn this lesson the hard way.

It's a myth that self-care will take you away from achieving your goals and revenue because you're taking time to work out or take a walk in the park. My three-month burnout cost me time and sales. My three-month burn-out showed me what selling from fear looks like and I swore never to go back there again. I made a conscious choice to say yes to self-care first and work second. If selling more meant I couldn't have time to journal, exercise, meditate, or hang out on my farm with my family, then something had to change. Instead of taking on every client and every speaking and training event, I became selective, hired a team, and increased my fees. What I was now saying yes to was my value, my impact, and my time. I was choosing to honor and love myself with self-care and my true worth.

Sign a PACT: Give Yourself Permission to Act with Compassion and Trust

Let's go back to that part of your brain that's wired to keep you safe and doesn't like the unknown. It prefers certainty, familiarity, and the known. These characteristics instill safety. Any actions you take that lead you away from this place of safety alert this part of your brain, notifying it you've ventured out of your comfort zone. It now takes the lead to take you back into your comfort and safety zone, back into the familiar. We also know that selling is not always going to be comfortable or easy. At times, you may be aware that you're selling from fear and you still need to move forward. This is your way through.

I was coming to the end of my three-month burnout recovery state and an opportunity to propose a sales training program for a group of professionals arose. Even though I was moving closer to a state where I could sell from love, I still had threads of fear permeating through my mind, heart, and body. I wasn't yet fully on the other side of the line, aligned to selling from love. Yet I had this opportunity I wanted to go for. So, how do you sell when you know you're not in a state to sell from love but are still working from fear?

You give yourself **P**ermission to **A**ct with **C**ompassion and **T**rust. You make a pact with yourself that no matter how bad the sales presentation goes, no matter how much fear you feel the moment you hit publish on your LinkedIn article, and no matter how much the urge to prove you're worthy of a client takes over your conversation, you will give yourself permission to move forward and take action. Regardless of the outcome, you will still have compassion and kindness towards yourself, and trust that no matter what happens you know you are creative, capable, and competent enough to handle it.

I signed this PACT before I went in to make my sales presentation to the executive running the department. I was afraid and flooded with doubt in the days leading up to my meeting. I knew I was still deep in fear, not fully back to health, and repeatedly questioned why I was putting myself in this situation. I must be crazy! I'd go on runs to move all the anxious energy out while repeating over and over again, out loud (I live in the country, so no one's around to see this), "I give myself permission to act with compassion and trust." Every time I recited these words, the fear lessened, my doubt diminished.

We sell from fear when we don't sell. Selling from fear will hold you back from selling anything at all. Even when you feel fear, but you move forward with the intention to use your Brilliant Difference to serve and add value, with compassion and love towards yourself and your client, you are still selling from love.

My fear didn't fully dissipate before my big sales presentation. I was excited about this work: I knew the program I was proposing would help them increase confidence, sales, and revenue. I wanted to use my Brilliant Difference to help them get what they most wanted. My presentation wasn't my best performance—I did stumble, and I made some mistakes. I got a whole lot right too. I focused on my client, asked for feedback, listened, and dug deeper to understand what they needed and wanted. My sales presentation and program proposal were not perfect. But through our conversation we were able to make some changes that would make it perfect for them. They said yes.

If I had succumbed to selling from fear, I would not have moved forward and definitely wouldn't have had the opportunity to work with this client and team. Giving myself permission, the okay, that even if it's not okay I'll be okay, worked, and it will work for you too.

This Permission to Act with Compassion and Trust is a guiding practice that will help you move forward to sell your products and services, post blogs, launch a podcast, speak on stage, and say yes to clients you think are too big for you, and even ask for fees that make you cringe. This is a personal commitment contract that will help you move from fear, uncertainty, and doubt to compassion, trust, and love.

You can use PACT as a mantra, for those moments when you know you are selling from fear or about to enter the zone. Repeat to yourself: *I give myself permission to act with compassion and trust.* Or, here's a Permission to Act with Compassion and Trust Contract for you to read, sign, and use every time fear creeps in, to remind yourself of your intention to use your Brilliant Difference to serve.

PERMISSION TO ACT WITH COMPASSION AND TRUST COMMITMENT

I give myself permission to act with compassion and trust.

My intention is to use my Brilliant Difference to serve and add value.

I consciously choose to take the next best step forward with gentle care and kindness towards myself, as I would for my best friend.

Regardless of the outcome, I promise to continue to have compassion and love toward myself.

I trust that no matter what happens, I know I am creative and capable to handle it.

Even if I don't know what to do, what I do know is that I am confident in my ability to figure out what needs to be done. I have faith and trust in myself.

There is nothing outside of myself that can fill me up with value or worthiness.

I am already worthy and deserve happiness, success, fulfillment, and love.

I am willing to give myself Permission to Act with Compassion and Trust.

I choose to give myself Permission to Act with Compassion and Trust.

I believe I can give myself Permission to Act with Compassion and Trust.

I am giving myself Permission to Act with Compassion and Trust.

Date: Signature:

RECAP

Let's review before we move on:

In Part One: "Love Yourself", we talked about how important it is for you to love yourself to sell from love. You need to be authentic, love who you are, and bring your Brilliant Difference.

To bring more confidence and connection to your conversations you need to communicate clearly the value you bring and the impact it delivers. It's critical for you to find the words, not fly-by-the-seat-of-your-pants words, but words you deliberately and thoughtfully craft and love, to declare your Brilliant Difference.

Selling is not always easy and comfortable. You will be invited into situations that evoke fear, uncertainty, and doubt. That is to be expected because, when you sell from love, you'll be leaving your comfort zone and moving into your courage zone. This will unlock your highest potential and allow you to make a meaningful difference through your work.

With guiding self-love and self-care principles you are now equipped to bring your Brilliant Difference, move from comfort to courage and sell from love—even amid fear, uncertainty, and doubt.

As we close off Part One: "Love Yourself", selling from love reminds us to let go of scarcity, self-interest, criticism, inaction, and the heaviness that selling from fear brings. Instead, call forth the openness, authenticity, courage, and kindness that selling from love creates for you, your clients, and the world at large.

We're off to Part 2: "Love your Client", the second stage to sell from love, where you'll learn how hearing your clients' interests and seeing the world through their eyes not only transmutes selling from fear, but will transcend it.

PART TWO:

—

LOVE YOUR CLIENT

CHAPTER FIVE:
MASTER THE SELL FROM LOVE SKILLS

—

"The most important thing in communication is hearing what isn't said."

Peter Drucker

WHEN MEETING WITH clients, attending networking events, or expanding your reach on social media, there are four critical skills you need to connect authentically to your clients, uncover how you can truly serve them, and sell from love. Those skills are preparation, deep listening, asking questions with wonder and curiosity, and honoring the silence.

Each of these selling from love skills asks you to invest in your relationships, show up without judgement and assumptions, and be attentive and discerning. Most importantly, these skills invite you to be present in the moment with what is happening for you, for your client, and in your environment.

Being present is not always easy or comfortable. It's hard and takes conscious, deliberate effort. You live in a noisy, busy, distracted world where your days are filled with competing priorities, sales targets, and client requests. Your brand, reputation, and identity often feel at stake, defined by how you respond, perform, and deliver. All of this pulls you away from being present, making an ideal environment for selling from fear to enter. When you're not present, you're in your head, thinking about what you should say next to your client, what your client is thinking, how much you need this sale, how you'll handle the dreaded objection you're certain is coming, or how you'll present your fees. Or you're making up stories—your client isn't interested as they're not jumping out of their seat; your client doesn't have the money to pay your fees; your client is asking way too many questions; they don't trust you. You've ended up in the land of fear.

When you sell from love, you're present to what is, not what should be. You're alert and conscientious about what is going on for your client, rather than for you and what you want.

The desire to control the outcomes and results comes from fear, not love. When you sell from love you acknowledge and accept what is—at least more of the time. Being present is what enables you to access love. The superpower skills of preparation, deep listening, asking questions with wonder and curiosity, and honoring the pause in silence with your clients anchor you in the present and make it possible to sell from love. Fear cannot abide in presence.

Selling From Love Skill #1: Preparation, preparation, preparation

Real estate agents often say "location, location, location" when it comes to the choosing what real estate to buy. When selling from love, I want you to repeat "preparation, preparation, preparation." It's the best investment of time and effort you can make after self-care. Whether preparing for a client meeting, a networking event or conference, or writing an article for social media, the prep work you do will pay you dividends in self-confidence. It will help you create a strong connection to your client and help you navigate the uncertainties of marketing and selling your products, services, and expertise.

I had to learn this the hard way. It was still in the early days of my sales career. I had taken on a new portfolio of commercial banking clients and was arranging introductory meetings. I set up a meeting with a particular client whose business name sounded familiar, but I didn't know why, so I paid no attention to it. They only had a credit card with the bank so I assumed this would be an easy call as they didn't have complex banking needs and were probably a small mom-and-pop-shop type of business. Now you know what happens when you assume, right? Did I ever get it wrong.

I pulled up to their offices and their bright-white-with-blue-and-grey business name and logo were flashing before me. I finally knew why the name rang a bell. Their billboards were plastered across the city at major commercial developments and they were the primary contractor for the biggest airport in the country. They were not a micro business; they were massive. I had a holy crap moment. My heart began racing, my breath became frantic, and beads of sweat were forming under my arms: what was I going to do now?

I started imagining ways to get out of it. I even pondered having my assistant back at the office call the client to cancel our meeting as I'd unexpectedly fallen ill. It wouldn't have entirely been a lie—I was feeling sick, ready to vomit from the flood of fear I was experiencing. But I'm not built that way. I needed to muster up some courage, eat some humble pie, and head into their office.

It was the quickest and saddest definition of a client meeting anyone could have. The secretary guided me into the boardroom that was dressed in a grand, deep-red mahogany boardroom table with accompanying stately chairs. She invited me to take a seat and said, "They will be in to see you momentarily." "They?" I asked. To which she replied that the CEO and CFO would be joining me. I didn't know what to say or what to do. I looked toward the front bay windows to see if I could make a swift escape. The CEO and CFO entered the room. We exchanged pleasantries and then I pulled out the credit card application renewal form for them to sign. I left within five minutes of my arrival. These were the most torturous five minutes I've ever had with a client and the biggest lesson on preparation I'd learn in my career.

Preparation is not only about you, it's about your client too. My clients were expecting to have a thoughtful business conversation about their banking needs with their account manager. That didn't happen because I wasn't prepared. I didn't do my homework to prepare myself so that we could focus more on them and what they were looking for. Instead, the lack of preparation had me selling from fear and as a result getting in and out of their offices as fast as possible.

Preparation means doing your homework. Do a Google search of your prospective client, review their website, especially their "about" page. See what you can find out about their vision and values. Connect with them on LinkedIn. They may have a Facebook page or be on Instagram. There you'll find out what they like to do on weekends: are they family-oriented or ultra-marathoners; what excites them? All of this information tells you what's most important to your client, making it easier to focus genuinely on their priorities. It also helps make for good, quality conversations with them.

You don't want to get caught in the preparation trap. This is where you keep digging, keep researching, and never actually meet with them! Decide what "prepared enough" looks like for you. You need just enough to move forward to meeting with your client or attending the event. The rest you'll find out in time using the other selling from love skills.

Another aspect of preparation is setting an objective and outlining an agenda. You want to define what success looks like before you even start. Ask yourself, how will you know if the meeting or event was a success? How will you know it was a valuable and worthwhile use of your time and, more importantly, your client's time? Prior to any meetings, proposals, presentations, or promotions, ask yourself the following questions:

- What do you want your client/audience to know?

- What do you want your client/audience to do?

- What do you want your client/audience to feel?

What I love about these questions is that they give you a head, hands, and heart approach to your marketing and selling activities. First, this helps you see the perspective of your clients. You're focusing on them, one of the most important aspects you need to keep in mind when selling from love. Second, it gives you clarity on the objective and intention behind your actions. You're getting clear on the purpose and meaning behind your client meeting, proposal presentation, or the promotion plan of a new service.

When setting your agenda and objectives for your client meetings, you need to make sure you don't forget to ask your client what they want on the agenda. It's simple, but often something that's missed. You get so bogged down in preparing yourself and your presentation that you forget about the most important person, your client. An easy way is, when your meeting is set, to ask your client what they would like to discuss or what is most important to them that you cover at the meeting. Add it to your agenda and be sure to email it to your client in advance so that they know exactly what to expect at your meeting.

Here are a few great questions you can ask your client prior to every meeting or call you have. This makes it easy for you to set an objective for those spontaneous calls or for when you didn't have enough time to prepare or set an agenda.

- What would be most valuable and useful to you?

- What would you like to take away from our time together today?

- How will you know that the time we spent today was valuable and useful to you?

Finally, when preparing for a client call, presentation, or event, you need to consider what *you* need to stay anchored and confident. If you're meeting with a high-stakes client, perhaps taking a short walk outdoors will help you air out any nerves you're feeling and clear your head. If you're preparing to attend a networking event, and you're an introvert, you may want to limit how much socializing you do during the day, so you have ample energy to mingle in the evening at the event.

Preparation will help you be present with your client. If you're prepared and have an agenda, you won't be focused on you and what you're going to say. You can direct your attention to your client and what they are saying. Preparation will help you guide the conversation in a meaningful and personal way. Preparation means preparing your material, your agenda, and yourself so you can be focused on your objectives, keep your client in mind, and stay aligned to selling from love.

Selling From Love Skill #2: Deep listening

During a Brilliant Difference Brand workshop with a group of financial service professionals, Mark raised his hand and said, "I know my client's whole life story before they even find out my last name." The group was discussing how their zone of brilliance showed up in client interactions. Mark's Brilliant Difference showed up through listening. He had learned that listening, rather than speaking, was his most valuable tool to build connections, develop relationships, and get more sales.

Listening is underrated and undervalued. Typically, the overtly loud, boisterous, and extreme extroverted professional is viewed as the ideal salesperson. In Daniel Pink's *To Sell is Human*, he shares research that points to the contrary. Social scientists have found that there is no statistically significant correlation between sales and extraversion. Pink quotes another study where the researchers noted the most destructive behavior of sales professionals was "an excess of assertiveness and zeal that led to contacting customers too frequently."[1] In other words, talking too much and listening to little holds you back from making meaningful connections and from selling—period—but especially from selling from love. So, if you're an ambivert or an introvert, you've got an edge on the extroverts. And if you're an extrovert, no worries, deep listening will help you avoid getting caught in an "excess of assertiveness and zeal".

When you truly listen, you're not formulating an answer or thinking about what you will say next. For instance, you're not saying to yourself, 'What if they have an objective, how will I overcome it? It's getting close to the end of the meeting, I really should ask them to work with me. I can't wait to tell my team we just closed the big one." This type of listening is called listening to respond and it's a sign you're moving toward fear-based selling. Keep an eye out for it.

Listening can be one of the most difficult skills to master because as your client is speaking, your brain is doing what it does best: taking in the information, assessing it, and formulating ideas and solutions. This is a skill you can master, but you're going to need to be patient with yourself. Let's first talk about the various types of listening. Yes, there are degrees to how deeply and intimately you need to listen when selling from love:

- **Level One Listening**: Level one listening only hears what you are talking about to yourself. For example, during a conversation, your client tells you about their recent trip to Disney. Immediately, your mind gets distracted about the trip you took to Disney last year. You want to tell them about the meal you had at that phenomenal steakhouse. Then you start thinking about how you're going to ask them to sign up for a new fee-based service your company is offering.

- **Level Two Listening:** Level two listening hears your internal narrative and what your client is saying. Like a tennis match, you're ping-ponging back and forth: present to the voice inside your head and present to what your client is telling you. In level two listening, you notice when you're not present with your client. You become aware when you've dropped into level one listening. For example, as your client is talking about their Disney trip, you start thinking about the steakhouse your family visited and how you want to tell your client about it. Then you notice you're not listening to your client, so you refocus back on them, as they continue to rave about their trip to Disney. Then you get distracted by the anxiousness you're feeling because you're going to pitch the new fee-based service. And once again you notice that you've moved away from paying attention to your client and bring yourself back to focusing on them. Over time, as you improve how present you are, you'll also catch yourself sooner and more often.

- **Level Three Listening:** Level three listening occurs when you listen with your ears and with your body and intuition. This type of listening pays attention to the conversation you're having with your client, your inner monologue, and what's happening in the atmosphere. You notice the physical environment—perhaps as you're meeting with your client at their office, there's a group of colleagues celebrating in the lunchroom. You also notice what is not being said. You're paying attention to the nuances of what is happening between the words, body language, and the emotional tone of your client. For example, as your client is telling you their Disney story, you notice their facial expression changes when they mention their mother who went along with them on this family vacation. Because you're paying attention, you pick up on this and ask how their mom is doing. The client then opens up, telling you she recently had a stroke and is recovering, but her health and well-being are weighing on the family. Level three listening helps you hear what wants to be said but that your client is omitting or overlooking.

Okay, now that you have a picture of the different levels, here are some practical ways to practice:

1. Use eye contact as an anchor to bring you back to the present moment. Don't be weird and stare your client down; that's creepy. Keep it natural and connect enough to get out of your head and back on your client and to what they're saying or *not* saying.

2. Write as your client speaks. I find this one works well when you're doing phone or video calls rather than in-person meetings. But it doesn't mean you can't do it in person. Tell your client in advance of your conversation that you'll be taking notes to capture their priorities and requests. Write in bullet point form; keep it short and concise. Writing will keep your mind occupied and you'll get awesome notes for your files.

3. Connect to your body and breath. The voice in your head pulls you away from being present and listening. Getting out of your head by noticing your breath or feeling into your body are perfect vehicles to get you out of your head. For one, you're always breathing, and two, your body is always with you. You can't leave home without it.

4. Meditate. Not when you're with your client, that would probably freak them out. Start a meditation practice, even if for five to ten minutes a day. I recommend a concentration type practice where you set a timer and focus on your in and out breath. Every time you get distracted by your thoughts, as you would in a client meeting, the

practice of coming back to paying attention to your breath helps you remember to come back and pay attention to your client when your thoughts carry you away. Now you may be saying to yourself that you're not good at meditating. Every time you sit down to quiet your mind, you get distracted and your mind gets busy. Every time this happens, and you notice it, you are meditating. Noticing and catching yourself when you get busy in your head is exactly what you want to be doing. The more you do this, the less distracted you'll get, and the more you will increase your concentration abilities. This, in turn, increases your listening abilities, because meaningful listening comes from great focus.

Deep listening provides a strong foundation and supports the development of the next selling from love skill: asking questions with wonder and curiosity.

Selling From Love Skill #3: Asking questions with wonder and curiosity

"He who asks a question is a fool for five minutes; he who does not ask a question remains a fool forever."

Chinese Proverb

Being someone to whom clients turn for answers puts a lot of pressure on you. You feel pressure to know it all and be ready for whatever curve ball a client may throw your way. As a professional, you're expected to be a wealth of knowledge, resources, and expertise. They turn to you to get answers and to help them get unstuck and achieve their objectives. It's no wonder many get caught in the "I need to tell, show, and prove to you that I know my stuff" trap. This pressure to know it all can put you back on track to selling from fear.

Talking more and listening less is how fear gets the upper hand. Asking questions, in fear's view, is an act of not knowing. When you sell from fear, asking questions feels as though it might drive you further away from getting the sale because your client will see you don't know or have all the answers. Selling from fear takes over when you're worried about how you're being perceived. Your identity, your image, and your reputation are at risk. Selling from fear can cause worries about what impression you will leave on others.

All this pressure can be alleviated when you sell from love. When you sell from love, you realize that your competence and intelligence are not determined by how much you talk and tell. That your value and worthiness are not measured by how much you know. Selling from love is demonstrated by the interest, curiosity, and wonder you bring to your client conversations and interactions. When you sell from love, you remember that asking questions is your selling superpower. You know when you ask questions from a place of wonder and curiosity that you demonstrate to your client you are someone they can trust. They know you're honest and forthright and that you're someone they will be able to trust over the long haul.

Selling from love means asking questions with an intent to connect, understand, and serve. Let me repeat that if you missed it: selling from love means asking questions with an intent to connect, understand, and serve. To ask powerful questions you need to be present and grounded in the moment. Deep listening plays an integral role in the quality of questions you ask. Often when you're listening you can get caught up in level one listening, hearing only the narrative in your head. As a result, you not only miss out on hearing what your client is truly saying and what is going on for them, you miss out on the lift-off point—the point from where all your powerful, curious, wonder-based questions will come from. Your best questions come from picking up on what your client is putting down. They are not scripted or planned, they occur naturally, in the moment, because you're present with your client: no agenda, no ego.

Preparation and scripted open-ended questions are a good place to start your client conversation. These come in handy when you notice there's a chance for fear or one of the protection strategies, such as proving or pleasing, to emerge. There are four types of questions you could ask your client, each of them serving a specific purpose, each progressively improving your ability to connect with your client and discover more about how you can help them.

1. **Close-ended questions**: These questions are fact-finding, yes/no, decision-type inquires. They usually start with "do", "is", "will", or "have".

For example:

- Do you like this option?

- Will you move forward?

- Is this what you had planned?

- Have you thought more about my proposal?

  Close-ended questions are important, and part of your selling from love conversation. They give you quick answers; however, they can also slow down or close off a conversation. Hence, when selling from love, most of your time should be spent asking the next three types of questions.

2. **Open-ended questions**: These questions help you uncover more than the facts and give you insight and information regarding what is most important to your clients. Open-ended questions usually start with a "what" or "how". Here are a few examples of open-ended questions:

- What are your current goals and objectives?

- What have you done up to now to achieve them?

- What is most important to you right now? Why?

- How did you accomplish that? What worked? What didn't?

- How do you feel about your current situation? How would you like it to be or feel?

  Open-ended questions are short and to the point. You want your client to do most of the talking and framing your questions in a concise manner will turn the conversation back over to them.

3. **Follow-up questions**: These are the next most powerful questions you can ask. These questions arise from what your client says, doesn't say, or what you sense they want to say but haven't said yet. These types of questions are not scripted or planned. You ask them

because you are present and genuinely want to know more. These questions arise when you're in level two or level three listening. Take that moment when you notice their tone changes when they mention their mother during a family vacation. You pick up on that nuance and follow up with a thoughtful, deeper, probing question. Follow-up questions are inspired by wonder and curiosity. These questions are often discounted and dismissed when they first occur to you. These questions help you uncover what is happening below the waterline. They help you clarify what is not clear enough and needs inquiry and further examination.

4. **Wonder questions:** Wonder questions are the most powerful questions you could ask yourself or your client. Wonder puts you in a state of unknowingness, openness, and curiosity. When you start a question with "I wonder", you immediately put yourself in a position of inquiry and demonstrate a thirst to know. Judgments and assumptions are instantly released. You can bluntly ask your client a question that includes the word "wonder", or you could start with "I wonder" in your mind and then follow through, out loud, with the question to your client. Here are ten simple, open, curious, wonder questions you could include in your client meetings:

    1. I wonder what do you want?
    2. I wonder what you really want?
    3. I wonder what is important to you?
    4. I wonder what a positive outcome looks like for you? Feel like for you?
    5. I wonder what your current state is?
    6. I wonder what is standing in your way?
    7. I wonder what possible steps you could take?
    8. I wonder what is the best next step?
    9. I wonder what support you need?
    10. I wonder how I could help?

Another great way to use wonder questions is in client meetings when you have no clue as to what to ask next. Say out loud, "I wonder…" and pause to see what question pops into your mind that wants to be asked. It's risky but don't worry; trust that a brilliant question will appear. When you trust yourself enough to put yourself at risk in this way, you know you are selling from love.

Selling From Love Skill #4: Sitting in silence and honoring the pause

There is an opportunity, both for yourself and the client, in pausing to allow time for reflection and processing in your conversation. There is a power in the pause. Having the ability to sit in silence is selling from love. When you're afraid, it's very difficult to pause. You fear silence because silence is filled with the unknown, which triggers even more fear. Learning to sit in the pause, the silent moments between your client's words and reactions, is a key skill in your selling from love toolkit.

Earlier we looked at meditation as a practice to help you improve concentration, focus, and listening. Meditation is a silent activity. There is no talking, only paying attention, perhaps attention to the discomfort of just sitting there, doing nothing. This is hard for many of us to do in our busy, always-on-the-go state of mind. No wonder we have a hard time doing it when working with clients. Meditation will help you improve your ability to sit and stay with the thoughts, feelings, and the urges to say something. Meditation will help you honor the pause and sit in silence and sell from love using this master love skill.

I was working with a sales leader, Bryan, as he was coaching one of his employees, Jennifer. My role was to observe his coaching as he tried to help Jennifer improve her sales results. The coaching session was going well and then he asked a very powerful, open-ended, curious question:

"Jennifer, what held you back?"

Jennifer's face immediately changed. Her eyes glazed over and turned upwards.

Bryan, thinking she didn't understand the question, responded with that kneejerk reaction we can sometimes get: he rapidly asked her a series of questions. In other words, the "cluster questions": "What I mean is would it have made it easier if Sam was there? What would you have done if he was there? What would have helped you make the ask? Did you need more information on the product?"

Jennifer not only ignored Bryan's first powerful question, but also the following three open-ended questions and proceeded to respond only to the last close-ended question. Bryan didn't feel comfortable in the pause, allowing Jennifer to look for an answer to his "what held you back?" powerful question. This discomfort was fear that ended up having him assume lack of product knowledge is what held Jennifer back from asking the client for their business. This very well could have been one of the reasons, but Jennifer and Bryan will never know because the fear Bryan was experiencing was too strong to allow him to sit in silence.

After Jennifer left, and in our debrief, I asked Bryan why he added more questions to his already excellent question. He said, "She looked like a deer in headlights! I thought I needed to help her out with more clarifying questions."

Bryan was uncomfortable with silence. He could not sit in the quiet while Jennifer processed his question. His thoughtful question was probably challenging her in some way. He felt discomfort for putting her in this uncomfortable situation. To make things better, he went in to save her from the pain of the supposed misunderstood question. However, Jennifer had understood the question. She was thinking.

When you ask someone a powerful, thoughtful question, they often need time to find the answer, to go inside and reflect. Asking open-ended, follow-up, or wonder questions requires you to make room for your client to think and process. You're creating a gateway for them to have an "aha'" moment.[2]

David Rock, the cofounder of the Neuroleadership Institute, a consultant, and the author of *Your Brain at Work,* describes an "aha" moment like this: "…'aha!' moments that spark brilliant, unexpected solutions tend to crop up when our minds are quiet and our consciousness is at rest.[3] These aha moments are often the only way to solve truly complex problems that are too big for our conscious mind to process."

When working with your clients, or your team if you're a sales leader, you want quiet, pause, and time for reflection and processing in all your conversations. The silence gives room for thinking and feeling to happen so that your client can have an insight or moment of discovery.

When we're asked a powerful question or we are looking to solve a complex problem or thinking deeply, our eyes will do a funny thing. It was what Bryan described as the "deer in headlights" look. What really happens is our eyes turn upwards—towards our brain. It's not a sign that your clients are confused or misunderstood, it's actually that they're using their eyes to look for the answer up in their head. In other words, you *want* your clients to have a "deer in headlights" look. It's a sign you're on the right track. To honor the pause and sit in silence:

1. Don't jump in to interrupt your client's thinking and processing time.

2. Be quiet and honor the pause, giving them this gift of love to think, process, and feel what they need.

3. If you notice the urge to fill in the silence with words—hesitate, count to three, and observe the sensations going on in your mind and body as you want to fill the gap.

4. Ask your client your powerful question and then add, "I'll give you some time to think about this" or "take your time". You're giving your client permission to slow down and setting yourself up to pause with more comfort and ease. You're acknowledging the value of being thoughtful.

CHAPTER SIX:
FALL IN LOVE WITH YOUR CLIENT

—

"The more we are concerned with the well being of others, the closer we will feel to each other."

Dalai Lama

WHEN YOU SELL, there are two things going on simultaneously. There's the value your client is getting because you're helping them solve a problem and there's what you're getting: compensation, recognition, accolades, and revenue. You willingly offer your products, services, and expertise to solve your client's problems and help them achieve their goals. Your clients willingly offer you compensation so you will help them get what they want. You're giving them something and, in exchange, they are giving something to you. However, it gets messy if the sale defines who you are and who you are not.

There's nothing wrong with having an investment in making the sale. It's normal; and who doesn't want to make money, increase market share, or get more clients? But when you get attached and create a personalized invest-ment in the sale, that's when you might start selling from fear.

It's one thing to want to succeed and another to bind your identity and worth to your success.

When you define who you are by how much you sell, you attribute more significance and value to the sale than to yourself. You start to matter less than your sales record. And then what do you do? You seek to feel better about your self-worth by falling back into hustling and earning your way, aka selling from fear. Let me share a story to illustrate.

I had worked with Tara on a previous project where I delivered a leadership personal branding workshop to her company. Tara is the program manager for a global company's learning and development team. There was a new senior executive team forming and they were looking for someone to con-duct a team-building workshop. Tara invited me to submit a proposal. After a bit of back and forth, we agreed on the terms of the proposal and that's when Tara told me that I'd be meeting with the director of human resources, Kim, for the next level of approval.

Tara prepped me for my meeting with Kim, letting me know to come pre-pared with case studies on how my work had impacted team dynamics, lead-ership and, of course, my client's bottom line. As I prepared, I noticed I was becoming more tense, holding my breath, feverishly reviewing past client testimonials, program evaluations, and training outcome reports. I checked in with myself and realized a few things were going on.

Selling from fear was emerging. I was anxious and worried. What if Kim doesn't approve? What if they don't hire me? I noticed the protector strategies of proving and pleasing poking their pesky heads up. I wanted to prove I was worthy of doing this work with a client at this level. I didn't want to let Tara down; she'd spoken so highly of me to her team and to Kim, and I didn't want to disappoint her. I was anxious because I was unsure of what they were expecting from me and was making up a story that I may not be enough. I was bingeing on FUDGE!

Can you see how selling from fear starts? When I attached my self-worth to making this sale, I got lost. I was associating my value and my identity with whether or not they hired me or liked me. It can be subtle and hard to detect, but as you get familiar with the internal feelings and signs, it gets much easier to catch yourself. No matter how long you've been in business, selling from fear will always crop up. But luckily, selling from love will always offer you a beautiful pathway out.

I had only a few hours before my call with Kim and so I took immediate action to get back to selling from love. I started with reframing my self-talk. I used the positive power-primer self-talk exercise from Chapter 4. I set an intention for how I wanted the meeting to go and how I wanted to feel as a result. Then, using the voice of my inner champion, I repeated how I wanted the meeting with Kim to proceed:

- I am <u>willing</u> to have an authentic, genuine, and confident meeting.

- I <u>choose</u> to have an authentic, genuine, and confident meeting.

- I <u>believe</u> I can have an authentic, genuine, and confident meeting.

- I <u>am</u> having an authentic, genuine, and confident meeting.

Next, I needed to move the icky, fearful energy out of my body. I put on my runners, got my German short-haired pointer, Charlie, and we went out for a quick thirty-minute run. By the end of my run, I had moved the energy of fear and realigned myself with love. I felt reconnected to my purpose, my true worth, and I was no longer attached to what Kim or Tara thought of me or my work. I remembered that my value and worth are never dependent on anyone's perception of me or my performance. I was good enough, no matter if we worked together or not. Attachment to the outcome of this meeting was transmuted into inner peace and confidence. The meeting went off without a hitch and HR approved my proposal.

Now, self-talk and self-care can only take you so far when it comes to selling from love. What happened next required me to pull out the big love to win against the persistent effort fear was exerting on me.

Expand Your Love: Make it Bigger Than You

The company informed me I had one more meeting. It was with the big boss and he would provide the final sign-off for my contract. What? I had to go through this again?! Selling from fear can feel like a relentless force you have to overcome, always threatening to overwhelm and stop you.

In preparation for my meeting with the big boss, Mike, I checked him out on LinkedIn. I wanted to see what common ground we shared and if there was a way we could connect to build rapport. I learned that he was uber smart. He graduated from Harvard. Harvard! That sent me into a tizzy. Suddenly my sense of not being smart enough, capable enough, or good enough to work with this client was back and the alarm bells were ringing.

Then I did more research and learned I was going to run this workshop—if it ever got approved—for an audience that included a TEDx speaker, a best-selling author, a super successful entrepreneur, a senior partner from one of the biggest global corporate consulting firms, and a person whose name ended in "III". Who did I think I was that I could be good enough for this crowd?

I was moving further away from selling from love and going deep down the rabbit hole of selling from fear. Instead of focusing on my client and their needs, I got wrapped up in my interests and identity. I worriedly asked myself, *what will they think of me? Will I get it? Who do I think I am for even trying?* This is the work of selling from fear. It seeks self-preservation. I wasn't in any physical danger, but selling from fear put my identity at risk, which felt exactly the same. I desperately needed to save myself or I would not get an opportunity to work with this incredible client.

The big love I needed was to turn away from focusing on myself. I needed to turn towards my client and the love I felt for them. I needed to fall in love with my client. Falling in love with your client is about genuinely caring about their best interests. It's about putting their concerns ahead of your own, especially your own insecurities, but also your own desire to make money or gain recognition. You fall in love with your client when you see them through a lens of compassion and when you see them with a deep desire to serve. You see your client as a human being who is struggling with a specific problem and you see yourself as having the means to help solve it. That's exactly what I did. I shifted the focus off me, what they thought of me, and what I would get if it all worked out; I shifted the focus onto Mike, his team, and what they would get as a result of this workshop.

It worked! I showed up with natural confidence, with no need to prove that I was worthy or a desire to please so they would like me. I focused on their interests and the transformation Mike and his team would get as a result of the workshop we'd be doing. Transferring my attention and the focus of the conversation to what was in it for them instead of what was in it for me was the shift I needed to get invited to work with Mike and his team.

Everyone's Favorite Radio Station is WIIFM (What's in it for me?)

To fall in love with your client you need to start by dialing into their frequency. Selling from fear limits and narrows your point of view—its aim is to satisfy your interests, especially your ego. As a result, it dials into your favorite radio station: WIIFM or "What's in it for me?" This is completely normal. It's part of why you're selling your products, services, and expertise. You are getting something out of the deal, be it a new car or the money to cover school tuition for your kids. There will *always* be a WIIFM station in your head. However, we have to turn down the volume, or we forget our clients. For instance:

- If you're an accountant, when you're dialed into WIIFM you'll focus on if your client will think *you* have enough experience to help them build cash flow. You'll forget that your guidance is there to help your client improve cash flow so he can pay his employees on time.

- If you're a real estate agent and WIIFM is blasting, you'll focus more on getting your client to sign *you* as their listing agent so *you* can meet quota. You'll forget that finding your clients their new home will provide them with more family time by living closer to work and spending less time commuting.

- If you're a business consultant and WIIFM is all you're listening to, you'll focus on the industry recognition *you'll* get by adding this big new client to your roster. You'll forget that your strategies will provide your clients with the tools to execute their projects on time and within budget.

To move away from selling from fear and back to love you need to turn down the volume on WIIFM and turn up the volume on WIIFT, "What's in it for them?" You remember and reconnect to the reason you're selling what you're selling and to whom you're selling to.

Switching from WIIFM to WIIFT shifts your perspective. You'll ease up on believing your self-worth is at stake with this sale and you'll tap back into your why. You're not only selling to make money, get accolades, and feel the rush of hitting your sales targets; you're selling to help people solve their problems and transform their lives, and to make a meaningful difference in the world.

The following exercise will assist you in switching channels. Before every high-stakes situation, when fear has a good chance of messing with your marketing and sales efforts, do this exercise. Whether it's before a discovery meeting, before submitting a proposal, or before asking a client to work with you, this exercise will help you fall in love with your client and move the dial from WIIFM to WIIFT.

Make two columns.

>Column 1: What's in it for me?

>Column 2: What's in it for them?

Let's use my opportunity with Mike. In preparation for my call with him, here's my list:

WIIFM: What's in it for me?	WIIFT: What's in it for them?
• Make a difference and add value • Increase revenue and hit sales goals • Make money • Cover costs for new barn for our horses • Take my family on a vacation	• Mike will learn how to improve his communication and leadership style • He will learn how to tap into his team's full potential • Mike and his team will better understand each other and the value each brings • The team will learn how to communicate and work better together • The team will learn how to use their Brilliant Difference collaboratively • As a team they will deliver their initiatives with connection, enthusiasm, and success

Working through this exercise helped me remember that a sale had no inherent power to change my self-worth. It reminded me that I had expertise that could help my clients connect, communicate, and work better together. It took me out of the "not enough" narrative and tuned me into the challenges and goals Mike had for his team and the transformation he was seeking. I felt better and I fell in love with my client even more. When we are aligned and sell from love, we feel it!

Put Yourself in Your Client's Shoes: a Practical Empathy Exercise

In 2017, I was speaking at a financial adviser sales conference on empathy and how to think like a client. The advisers were responsible for helping small to mid-sized businesses with loans and lines of credit. They had aggressive sales targets. These advisers weren't business owners or entrepreneurs. They were employed, and with certainty and confidence they knew every two weeks their paycheques would be deposited into their accounts. This was one thing that wasn't keeping them up at night.

Alternatively, their client, a business owner who employs a staff of fifty, not only has to worry about putting food on her table, she also has the added pressure to ensure this happens for her fifty employees. If one of her clients fails to pay on time or a sale doesn't close, that puts her cash flow at risk. This will keep her up at night wondering how she'll meet payroll in two weeks. As financial advisers, their stresses and pressures are completely different than those of the business owners they are serving.

Moving the dial from WIIFM is an entry point; however, to truly understand and love your client in a deeper and more meaningful way, you need to learn how to see the world from their point of view. Seeing the world through their eyes will help you uncover a breadth of love you hold for them, which will in turn create a deeper, more caring, understanding relationship with your clients.

Empathy is having the ability to see the world through someone else's eyes, the ability to connect at an emotional level with deep understanding of what that other person is experiencing. Falling in love with your client means that you need to use your empathy muscles to understand and emotionally connect to:

- the challenges, frustrations, and pain they're experiencing

- the goals and dreams they're striving for

- the needs and values they hold most dear

When you do this, you expand the capacity to love your clients genuinely, and then selling from love is inevitable. When you truly connect with a client at this level, you connect to their deepest desires, hopes, and dreams. It's from this place of deep connection, through empathy, that you sell from love. How do you truly connect and understand what someone is going through, when you've not walked a mile in their shoes?

You're going to encounter all sorts of clients, coming from different backgrounds and situations, people who are like you and those that are completely different from you. To sell from love doesn't mean you can't work with them or that you need to figure out how to become a financial adviser-turned-entrepreneur to see the world through their eyes. Rather you need to meet them where they're at and, if you haven't walked in a mile in their shoes, this can be challenging. Don't fret, you can totally do this and here's a practical and powerful empathy exercise to show you just how. This exercise will help you see their point of view so that you can understand and connect to what they are experiencing and what is most important to them.

Back at the financial adviser sales conference, I invited the three-hundred-person room to stand up and practice thinking like a client using this empathy exercise. We began with this scenario:

"You're preparing for a client meeting. It's an existing client who recently purchased a shopping mall property, and you're aware that there has been increased vacancy at the mall, plus the loss of a major tenant. As you're preparing, you ask: What is top of mind for you? What's most important to you? What are you most concerned about? How will you know your meeting was a success?"

The advisers captured their responses and identified what they were thinking and feeling as they were preparing for this meeting. Top of mind were things like: "I need to get updated financial statements and rent roll of current mall tenants. I'm worried that we won't be able to accommodate my client and I'm concerned how I'm going tell them. I'm still so new to this portfolio and this is my first meeting with the client; this is not a good way to start a relationship. I fear that they'll be defensive and point to me as the bad guy or the new guy who doesn't know how to do my job. I am so stressed and am not looking forward to this meeting." As you can see, a lot was going on for them—and are you sensing the focus is dialed into WIIFM?

Next, they were invited to step out of their perspective by taking one step forward and now imagining they stepped into the perspective of their client. More information was offered:

"As the client, you recently have taken over the family business, founded by your grandfather, whose wish was to keep the business in the family. You're worried that the bank will call in the loan, and you don't have enough experience to feel confident about how to improve this financial situation. You also wish you had someone to talk to as a sounding board. Now, from this perspective, standing in your client's shoes, ask yourself: What is important to you as the client? What are you thinking and feeling? What are you most concerned about? What would make this meeting a success for you?"

As they stood in their client's perspective, they identified what was most important to their client and what they were thinking and feeling. Here's what standing in their client's shoes revealed: "I don't want to disappoint my family as they've given this huge responsibility to me. I'm overwhelmed with all my responsibilities and don't know where to start. I just graduated from university and am running this big business and have this scary meeting with the big bank. I really wish I had a trusted adviser that I could rely on and be open and frank with. I must play my cards and be sure not to tell them too much." The advisers had more information; by standing in their client's perspective their point of view expanded.

Next, they were invited to step out of their client's perspective by taking one step to the left and now imagining they stepped into the position of a bird's-eye view. They needed to imagine they were hovering over themselves (the adviser) and the client in the meeting: what could they see from this perspective? From this bird's-eye or "helicopter" perspective, they were invited to think about the following: "What do you notice going on in their world as you observe them from afar? What do you notice is the most important thing going on? What do you notice as the biggest concern? What do you notice regarding how they can make this meeting a success?"

The helicopter perspective offered more insights and information: "Both the adviser and client are focused on what is in the best interest of themselves and not for each other. From this view it looks like they both want to maintain a relationship with each other. The financial adviser wants to be the client's trusted adviser and the client wants one. However, they're so caught up in fear and worry that there is no space for this true desire to come up. To make this meeting a success, they need to honor what they each want but, more importantly, they need to put the problem out in front of them so that they can look at solving it together." At this point the room felt charged with enlightened excitement.

But we weren't done yet. In the final part of this empathy exercise I invited everyone in the room to step out of the helicopter perspective by taking one step back to the original position, with them as the adviser, and to respond to the following: "What do you notice now about this perspective? What new information or insight do you have? What will you do with the new insights?"

By this point the room was buzzing and I sensed the "aha" bubbles bursting everywhere. The energy was positive and palpable. There were giggles and "you got me" energy swirling as they learned and saw something that they hadn't considered before. From this final perspective, here's what they were able to see: "As the financial adviser I can appreciate that the client is feeling fear and uncertainty as they are coming to this meeting with me. I can see that my job is to build comfort with them. They need a trusted adviser and I want to be that for them. I want to guide, inform, and educate them through this challenge. We both want a positive outcome and I want to use this meeting to build trust, provide advice, and design what a success would be for the both of us in this situation."

For a moment, these financial advisers got to step into the shoes of their clients to understand what the world looks like and feels like from their point of view. The helicopter perspective pulled them out of their interest and the client's interest and enabled them to notice what was happening in the environment and in the adviser-client relationship. Then, once they had a chance to come back into their original position, their adviser perspective, they had an expanded view, a true understanding and love for their client that was not there before this exercise.

When you step inside your client's shoes you see the world through their eyes. It allows you to understand deeply, to connect and fall in love with who they are. As Maya Angelou so eloquently said, "I've learned that people will forget what you said, people will forget what you did, but people will never forget how you made them feel."

It's through empathy that you fall in love with your client and that is the feeling they will never forget you made them feel.

The Selling from Love Client Empathy Exercise and WIIFM and WIIFT Exercise you learned about earlier are both included in the Sell From Love Workbook you can download at www.sellfromlove/workbook.

CHAPTER SEVEN:
LOVE THE TRANSFORMATION,
NOT ONLY THE TRANSACTION

—

"When we quit thinking primarily about ourselves and our own self preservation, we undergo a truly heroic transformation of consciousness."

Joseph Campbell

What Are You Really Selling?

YOU *THINK* YOU'RE selling a mutual fund, a leadership training workshop, dental supplies, or a business strategy to your client—but you're not. What you're really selling is the thing your mutual fund, workshop, dental supplies, or business strategy will *give* your client.

Here's the thing—your client doesn't care about your product, service, or expertise. The thing you are selling—the product, service or expertise—is the *transaction*. This is often where professionals get stuck. You are so enthralled with what you are offering that you forget why your client wants what you're offering in the first place. What your client cares most about is the outcome or result your offer will get them. This is the transformation. When selling from love the question you are asking yourself is *what change will my client get as a result?* That is what you are actually selling.

Here is something I have learned that has completely transformed how I do business: *they don't care about your stuff; they care how your stuff will help them get their stuff.*

One of the best examples I've come across is from Harvard marketing professor Theodore Levitt where he famously said, "People don't want to buy a quarter-inch drill bit. They want a quarter-inch hole."[1] A customer walks into a hardware store looking to buy a drill. Now, as the salesperson, you're thinking he wants a drill. Indeed, he does, but he doesn't really want the drill. What he wants is what the drill will give him. You see, he wants to put a shelf on his wall so he can display a few family photos and an award he recently received. Now you're thinking he wants to buy the drill to make holes so he can put up a shelf. It goes deeper than this. He wants the drill to put up the shelf to display his family photos and his award so he can be reminded of the connection and love he feels towards his family and the significance and leadership he contributed to his industry.

It's not the drill he's really buying. Your client is buying what the drill does. The drill gives him holes for a shelf, which then gives him a way to celebrate and validate who he is and the life he has. As a professional, you love your transaction, because it's the special thing you have to help your clients. It's the offer, the product, service, or expertise you bring to help facilitate the transformation your client wants. It's okay to love the transaction but, when selling from love, it cannot come at the expense of not acknowledging the transformation. You need to love the transformation even more than the product, service, or expertise you use to help your clients. When you do this, you are selling from love.

Here are a few examples of shifting from focusing on the transaction to the transformation:

If you're a workshop leader, you talk less about what will happen in the workshop and describing the content and the exercises, and focus more on what will happen as a result of the training, things like "Your team will communicate better, improve their relationships and, as a result, deliver their best performance on a current project."

If you're a financial adviser, you talk less about the product features of the mutual fund, where it's invested, the types of stocks and bonds, and talk more about the peace of mind your clients will have knowing that they will have a retirement fund with the appropriate level of risk to support their lifestyle.

If you sell dental supplies, you talk less about the price discounts available when your client buys in bulk or if they bundle their purchase with additional products and say more about the one-of-a-kind experience their patients will get because the tools they use are gentle, non-invasive, and reduce anxiety.

The transactional details such as the product features, process, and price are important, but if you make it centre stage, you will lose your client. Your client can't get excited about all the bells and whistles that come with your offer till they know and understand the transformation they'll receive as a result of it.

Empathy is at the Core of Transformation

Selling from love is an exchange of empathy, value, and love for something greater than the sum of its parts. Using our holes and drills example, selling from love is about what the drill ultimately gives your client, which is the connection, love, and significance he gets to experience (the transformation) as a result of buying the drill (the transaction).

The questions you endeavour to answer when you sell the transformation are:

- How will your client *feel* as a result of working with you?

- Who will your client *be* as a result of working with you?

- What will your client be able to *do* as a result of working with you?

- What will your client *have* as a result of working with you?

This is the transformation your client will feel, be, do, and have because they choose to work with you. This is the difference you make that is included in your Brilliant Difference. Recall in Chapter 2 where you crafted your Brilliant Difference Story. The difference component of your Brilliant Difference included the people you work with, the change you create for them, and the results you help your clients achieve. This is the transformation you promise to facilitate for your clients. This is how your Brilliant Difference works—because of bringing your Brilliant Difference, your client receives the transformation they are seeking, and you get to make a meaningful difference serving them. Now all you need to do is uncover the transformation they are looking for and demonstrate how your product, service, or expertise will help them get there.

The Four Transformations Your Clients are Seeking

When selling from love you must realize that you are not the person making the transformation happen. Your client is responsible for that. When you place yourself as the star of your client's transformation, that is selling from fear. Selling from fear focuses on you being the hero who came to save your client from the problems and hardships they are experiencing. When selling from love, it's not for you to save the day; it's your client. Your client is the hero and star of their own story. They make the decision to change, they take the necessary actions, they ultimately benefit from the changes they choose to make.

You'll notice fear emerge in your client's transformation when your identity, worth, and value are invested in the outcomes your client achieves as a result of working with you. For example, a financial adviser prepares a financial plan that their client follows to a T. By the end of the year they are debt-free and have three months' worth of salary saved in their bank account. Now if the financial adviser believed that he was the one that did that, that would be selling from fear. The financial plan and the guidance he provided facilitated the change for this client. But really, it was the client who managed the cash flow, said no to frivolous spending, and said yes to putting money away towards an emergency fund. The client is the hero, not the financial adviser.

The adviser played an important role—it was through his advice, guidance, and expertise that his client was able to achieve their goals. He acted as the facilitator and his clients delivered on the transformation. To sell from love your role is to facilitate change, but your role is not to make the change for your clients. You are walking alongside them, guiding, championing, and coaching them all the way through.

You do play an important role in your client's transformation. You, through your product, service, and expertise are the facilitator of their transformation. Your client needs you to provide a way for them to get what they most want. Using your offer, you guide them towards the transformation they are seeking. Holding yourself as a facilitator takes the responsibility away from you to make the transformation for your client. This lessens the chance of selling from fear to show up because the burden to make something happen falls on your client's shoulders and not yours. There's a lightness in knowing you are guiding and providing your client with a way to solve their problems, achieve their goals, honor their values, and fulfill their dreams, without feeling the need to do all the work to make the change happen for them.

There are four transformations you help facilitate for your clients:

Solving Problems - What is the problem they want to solve?

Achieving Goals - What is the goal they want to achieve?

Honoring Values - What is the value they want to honor?

Fulfilling Dreams - What is the specific dream they want to fulfill?

Let's take a deep dive into each of the transformations so you learn what you're looking for when facilitating a transformation for your clients.

Transformation #1: Facilitating change by helping your clients solve their problems

Transforming problems is typically the loudest and hottest transformation your clients want and are most likely to act on first. Your clients don't like to feel pain. They, like you, are pain-averse. They'll do whatever they can to make the pain go away. If you have a solution that will make their pain go away, you might just be the one your clients will choose to hire.

When looking to facilitate a transformation in this area, you are looking for specific pain points, challenges, or frustrations your clients are experiencing. These problems are keeping them up at night. They're worried about the impact these problems will have if they aren't solved. There is urgency for your client to take action to solve it immediately. Try any of the following questions to identify their pain:

- What current problem, challenge, or frustration are you experiencing?

- What have you done up to now to solve this problem, challenge, or frustration?

- What is keeping you up at night?

- What is your worst fear if this problem isn't solved?

- If this problem, challenge, or frustration were solved, what would life be like for you? What would it look like? What would it feel like?

You want to uncover the problems, challenges and frustrations they're experiencing so you can better understand how your offer will help them solve their problem, so they can get what they most want.

Maybe you're an HR consultant who helps companies support their employees' success by setting hiring practices, talent management strategies, and employee engagement initiatives. The problem your client is having is that they are growing so quickly that they're burning out staff, losing good people, can't hire fast enough, and don't have time to make plans for how to hire the right talent for the future. Your goal is to illustrate how using your company will make this problem go away and how your client will have happy, engaged employees and a talent pipeline of great people to hire. Imagine how at ease—and ready to work with you—your client will feel knowing this is the transformation your offer would facilitate for them.

Transformation #2: Facilitating change by helping your clients achieve their goals

With this transformation you are looking for the goals, objectives, and intentions your client wants to achieve. They want or need something and are striving to get it. Your product or service is the missing link. When they use your solution, they will get the thing they most want. If your client isn't focused on the problems they're having, they're usually focused on the goals they want to achieve. This is the second most urgent transformation your client is likely to want to create for themselves.

There are usually two types of people you'll come across: the people who are moving away from something or the people moving towards something. The people moving away are clients who most want the transformation of solving a problem. This is the first transformation we talked about. They want the bad thing they are experiencing to go away. The people moving towards something are clients who are seeking a transformation by achieving their goals. They want to create something they don't have.

Of course, everyone wants both the problems to go away and the goals to be fulfilled, but you need to uncover which one is your client's primary need: is it solving a problem or achieving a goal? What motivates your client the most: to take action to make something difficult go away or to take action to make something wonderful happen?

During your client conversations you're listening for the words they're using, their body language, and tone of voice. You're using your selling from love skills, the ones we talked about in Chapter 5. You're deep in level three listening and asking open, wonder-filled questions. For clients focused on Transformation #1 Solving a Problem, you'll notice negative language such as "don't", "stop", "worry", "prevent", "avoid", and "fix". Their shoulders and body may be curling forward, feeling tight and constricted. It's as though they're closing themselves off as a way to protect themselves. You'll also sense an urgency and rush to make this difficult experience go away. For clients focused on Transformation #2 Achieve a Goal, you'll notice more positive language such as "get", "start", "choice", "eager", "achieve", and "action". You'll notice an openness in their body language: they may hold their shoulders back and you sense they have an urge to move forward. Their tone of voice could be impatient, but not in a hurried state because of stress and worry, rather because there is enthusiasm to take action.

Imagine your business is helping people's digestion. Every time your customer eats, he gets a stomach ache and feels bloated and gassy. The person looking to solve a problem wants the discomfort to go away. He immediately reaches for Tums or Pepto-Bismol.

A customer who wants transformation by achieving a goal, doesn't want to experience the stomach ache ever again. The goal is to find a solution that ensures he no longer gets these stomach aches every time he eats. Instead of taking Tums, he consults with a naturopath and does a food elimination diet. He is willing to forgo immediate relief in order to achieve a goal of never having a stomach ache.

In certain areas of your life, you'd rather take the magic pill to make the pain go away and, in other situations, the further goal is more important and you'll bear the pain in order to achieve the goal. When working with your client, use the following questions to uncover their goals:

- What are your immediate goals? What are you looking to achieve in the next six to twelve months?

- What have you done till now to achieve this goal?

- What gets you up in the morning?

- What is your worst fear if this goal isn't achieved?

- If this goal were achieved, what would life be like for you? What would it look like? What would it feel like?

You are seeking to find the words your clients use to describe what they most want to be, do, and create in the near term. For example, I want to grow my market share and make more money, I want to get more clients and have more meaning in my life, or I want to get fit and flexible and feel confident and good in my skin. From there, you can more easily demonstrate how your offer can help achieve the goals that are most important to your client.

Transformation #3: Facilitating change by helping your clients honor their values

Values define who you are and what you live by. Your values determine what is most important to you. The same goes for your clients: they have a code of ethics or set of values that determine what they give importance to. These ethics serve as a guiding force in the decisions they make so they can live aligned to what they value most. When selling from love, your products, services, or expertise help your clients live out and actualize their values.

When engaging with clients, you're listening in to uncover their values. Values show up everywhere and it is not too hard to spot them. For example, during a conversation your client shares a story about how they left a company because they found it difficult to be themselves and that their work wasn't valued. You could conclude that a few of their values are authenticity, significance, and contribution. Then while visiting them at their office, you notice photos of family, their degrees, and their support in a local community event. In addition to the values you caught earlier, you make a good guess that they also value family, learning, and community. Then on their social media feed, you see posts about climate change and pictures of them canoeing and camping with friends. Considering this, you add nature and adventure to their value list.

When selling from love, your solution helps your clients honor their values. When your client is living in alignment to their values, life feels good, open, and filled with integrity. When they are not, then life feels hard, challenging, and exhausting. When you sell from love you're either helping them stay on track or you're helping them get back on track to honoring one or more of their values through your offer.

Take the client above who holds the values of authenticity, significance, contribution, family, learning, community, nature, and adventure; let's see how a financial adviser and a website designer would use their work to facilitate a transformation in helping this client honor their values.

Example 1: A financial adviser would focus on how a financial plan would help this client create a nest egg of savings to support their children through school and annual family vacations. This would help this client honor the values of family, learning, and adventure. They could make investment recommendations for ethical, sustainable, and environmentally conscious mutual funds that would speak to their values of nature and community.

Example 2: A website designer would help this client create a website that would attract customers and let customers make online purchases with ease so that the client had revenue coming in to support their family and lifestyle. They would build a website that made it simple enough for their client to post educational materials to share, no matter if they were on a beach in Costa Rica or in a cabin in the Rocky Mountains. This would help their client honor their values of authenticity, learning, significance, and adventure.

You need to demonstrate how your business will help your client honor their values. Your job is to uncover what they value and connect the dots so that they can see how working with you will help them live out what they hold most near and dear. When working with your client, you can use the following questions to uncover their values:

- What is most important to you?

- What do you value most? Why?

- Describe a time when you were on top of the world. What made it so meaningful?

- When was the last time you were irritated by someone or something? What happened?

- What activities do you most enjoy doing? Why?

Values show up everywhere, not only in your client conversations. In chapter five: "Master the Selling from Love Skills", we talked about preparation as an integral selling from love skill. When you're doing your homework to prepare for a client call or meeting, look for values on their website, social media feeds, and the internet. Use your senses and pay attention to what you see in their environment and what you hear in their voice when they talk about the things that are most important to them. When you understand their values, you then show them how working with you will help them honor those exact values.

Transformation #4: Facilitating change by helping your clients fulfill their dreams

The final selling from love transformation is facilitating a change by helping your clients fulfill their dreams. This is the richest and most fulfilling; at the same time, it is the transformation your client will more than likely focus on least. This one doesn't usually take the forefront because your client's dreams may feel so big or far-fetched—quitting their job, starting a business, moving to Europe, homeschooling their kids—that they dismiss them as even viable. Or they believe that they are too impossible to reach, such as creating a foundation to help save their community's old growth forest. Your clients stop before they even start.

The pain of not living out their dreams doesn't feel so bad in the present moment, either because they're making do with the daily grind of life or they're caught up in the busy-ness of life and don't even notice they're not living out their big dreams. Also, the gain and reward of living out a dream are so far into the future that having the grit to delay satisfaction in an instant-gratification world subdues the urgency to take action toward that dream. The dream then falls by the wayside, turning it into a 'someday I will' mantra.

Your job when selling from love is to uncover your client's dreams so that their dreams don't fall into the background or get buried under the busy to-do's of everyday life. When you take the time to identify your client's dreams, you're helping them mitigate the possibility of looking back on their life feeling filled with regret—those "shoulda's" and "woulda's". Selling from love reminds and awakens your client's dreams, reconnects them to their purpose, and re-energizes them to living a life that matters.

When selling from love, and to enable a client's transformation through fulfilling their dreams, here are questions you can ask:

- What would you do if you weren't afraid?

- If you had a magic wand and could have anything, what would you want?

- Out of curiosity, what did you want to be when you grew up?

- Imagine you're 95, looking back on your life: what would a life fully lived look like?

- Who inspires you? What is it about their life that inspires you?

- What legacy do you want to leave behind?

Now these may seem like big and deep questions to ask a client. You're worried that they're too personal or inappropriate to ask. These are important questions that your client may not even be thinking about. But by asking them, you help them start. They get to see that you care more about them, who they are, and who they want to be than the product or service you're proposing. They get to see that you care about them and that they're not a number because you take the time to ask personal, thoughtful, and yes, deep questions. I don't recommend you ask all of these questions all at once. One or two at a time, drop them in as they feel right, and acknowledge that it's probably going to be a courage zone moment for you to practice asking.

I recall a client who signed up for one of my coaching programs. She said that everything changed the day she heard me on stage ask her and the audience of two hundred other HR professionals "What would you do if you weren't afraid?" For her, it was to go back to school and get her MBA. That was two years ago. Today she is an MBA graduate fulfilling a lifelong dream that was hidden beneath the to-do's of her job, family, and life. That is the power of asking deep, thoughtful, and transformational questions. You have an opportunity to help your clients live out their dreams and experience powerful, life-changing transformations.

Carrying on from the previous example in the transformation of honoring values, the big dream this client has is to build a skin-care line that is nature-based, environmentally friendly, and supports sustainable farming. As a financial adviser, you'd demonstrate how your financial plan would help your client build cash flow and reserves that would enable them to invest in sustainable farming solutions, to support not only their product development but the community and industry as well. As a website designer, you'd show them how to make it easy for customers and their community to connect and contribute ideas and resources online to help invest in sustainable farming solutions, as this is the legacy and big vision they want to leave behind.

Selling from love is an act of service. You get to use your transaction, the product, service, or idea you're selling, to facilitate a change and transformation in your client's life or business. By loving the transformation, your clients don't feel like a number or as if you're using them to hit your sales goals. It stops being about you and becomes more about them. It's through this love that you get to bring more than a product to your client. You bring meaningful change, better outcomes, and the support to live out a more authentic life.

The Transaction is Inclusive; The Transformation is Exclusive

When selling from love you are not required to change who you are, what you offer, or the results you deliver. Using the selling from love transformations, you learn how to present yourself, the value you offer, and the difference you make in a personalized, empathetic way. Your client says yes to you because they feel heard. They know you are the best person to help them:

- Solve their problems

- Achieve their goals

- Honor their values

- Fulfill their dreams

I had the opportunity to sell from love to three different clients in a short period of time. Each client had unique problems, goals, values, and dreams, as each of your clients do too. Now if I had gone in talking about the transaction—my workshop and how amazing it was, all the things I'd be teaching, and the things they'd learn—I can guarantee you, I would not have had the opportunity to work with them. In addition, I only had one solution to offer, a team-building workshop to three very different clients. This was my Your Brilliant Difference Team Transformation workshop which helps teams identify what makes them unique so that they can use their individual strengths and differences to add value and grow their business.

As part of my Brilliant Difference, there were four changes this workshop promised to deliver. After this workshop participants could expect to:

1. Improve communication

2. Increase leadership and team effectiveness

3. Recognize untapped potential in current team members

4. Build trust and stronger relationships

Being clear on my Brilliant Difference and identifying the transformation the workshop delivered helped me connect, propose, and invite each of these clients to work with me. Each client was experiencing various problems and pursuing distinct dreams. They had different goals, unique values—and I only had this one workshop to offer. How do you take the one idea, product or service and create a personal, custom solution for your client? You take your inclusive transaction and make if feel like an exclusive transformation.

Communicating your Exclusive Transformation from Love

Here are three clients: Matt, Tina, and Jeff. Each is a leader in an organization with his or her own unique problems, goals, values, and dreams. During each discovery meeting, my objective was to understand what transformation each client was seeking. This would inform the best way to present and demonstrate how each would receive the outcome he or she was looking for. To illustrate that better for you, let's walk through each client transformation story.

Client 1: Matt Matt is the Senior Vice President for a Digital Transformation team for a financial services company. He leads a newly formed team of five executive leaders who have a big agenda and have a multi-million-dollar project budget. The team is diverse, ambitious, and filled with strong opinions on how to lead and execute on their mission. They are excited about the challenge but also feel the pressure to perform and deliver.

MATT – SVP Digital Transformation Team	
Transformation #1: Solving Problems	With a major influx of new peers, each with strong leadership styles, tension was brewing, and he is concerned about the silos forming on his team.
Transformation #2: Achieving Goals	To deliver on their two big projects with excellence, exceeding expectations so that they can drive significant customer growth and business value.
Transformation #3: Honoring Values	To have the ability to effect change and drive transformation. To add value and make a difference to customers and business. To be in a learning and growth environment while doing purposeful and meaningful work.
Transformation #4: Fulfilling Dreams	To create an organizational culture where they are all bonded in a "fellowship of the ring" mission.

Client 2: Tina Tina is the President and CEO of a F500 company. She leads a team of twelve executives for a company of 80,000 employees. Her company has been around for 150 years, faithfully holding to a stable, tried-and-true legacy and culture. Her executive team is seasoned, experienced, and have worked for the company or in the industry for twenty-plus years. The company is at a pivotal point in its industry. With a growing focus on automating and simplifying processes, their leadership is being invited to change and evolve with the times.

TINA - President and CEO of F500 Company	
Transformation #1: Solving Problems	They need to evolve the culture and leadership as new hires are coming in believing the company has a culture of innovation and passion; however, it's not yet being demonstrated by her leadership team.
Transformation #2: Achieving Goals	To create cultural norms that evolve the way they lead so that they can be open and flexible, and so they can maintain pace in a fast, ever-changing digital marketplace.
Transformation #3: Honoring Values	To focus on the customer; they always come first. Ensuring strong collaboration within the company to break down silos. Have a workplace that honors and invites diverse opinions, perspectives, and ideas.
Transformation #4: Fulfilling Dreams	To leverage the talent of a multi-generational leadership table; honor the legacy leadership style of the tried and true, while at the same time being open and receptive to the entrepreneurial leadership style of innovation and experimentation.

Client 3: Jeff Jeff is the CEO and founder of a technology start-up company. His company has grown quickly and recently had a significant injection of venture capital. The team has also grown considerably in the past six months, going from eleven employees to forty, and he is expecting it to grow further. The team has been uber-focused on a big project where they were all hands-on deck, working around the clock, with no reprieve for months. They've successfully delivered on this project. The team is multi-generational with seasoned, experienced leaders and highly ambitious new talent ready to move up the ladder quickly.

JEFF – Founder and CEO Tech Startup	
Transformation #1: Solving Problems	Currently they have an overworked team and quick growth in staff and are concerned about decreasing engagement. They work remotely and are concerned they'll lose engagement due to physical proximity or lose people to burnout.
Transformation #2: Achieving Goals	To focus on his people to reconnect and restore the team to stay healthy, work better together, and move forward on their business priorities effectively.
Transformation #3: Honoring Values	To stay true to their "start-up" culture while at the same time managing growth with a structure that doesn't infringe on company spirit. They want to continue to be agile, nimble, and to maintain pace in this fast and ever-changing marketplace.
Transformation #4: Fulfilling Dreams	To create a people culture program that supports the development of his people and is integrated into a process within the company so that they can onboard, recruit, and coach with ease.

Matt, Tina, and Jeff each had unique problems to solve, goals to achieve, values to honor, and dreams to fulfill. The next step was to take the transformations each were seeking and, using my offer (aka transaction), to demonstrate the difference it would deliver. The following template is a practical tool to help with just that.

Crafting your Selling from Love Transformation Story

This is the Selling from Love Transformation Story. Its purpose is to help you summarize the transformation your client is seeking in a simple and concise way, while encapsulating how your product, service, or expertise delivers the results your client wants. The script helps you focus your conversations on your clients and their priorities. The intent of this script is not for you to recite it word by word, but rather to help you stay connected to your client and to selling from love. There are five parts to the script. Four of them focus on your client and one on your offer.

Here's the template:

Currently you... State the problem your client wants solved.

You want to... State the goal your client wants to achieve.

YOUR DIFFERENCE(TRANSACTION): State your offer and the result it will deliver.

This is important to you because... State the values your client wants to honor.

Ultimately the intention is to help you... State the dreams your client wants to fulfill.

You identify your client's problems, goals, values, dreams, and then you plug them into each of the sentence starters. What you're left with is a simple, concise, empathetic message that is tailored in a manner that your client can hear and understand.

Let's take Matt, Tina, and Jeff through the Selling from Love Transformation Story.

MATT – SVP Digital Transformation Team	
Transformation	**Selling from Love Transformation Story**
PROBLEM	**Currently you...** have a major influx of new peers, each with strong leadership styles, tension is brewing, and silos are forming.
GOAL	**You want to...** deliver on your two big projects with excellence, exceed expectations so that you can drive significant customer and business value.
YOUR DIFFERENCE	This team building workshop will help you.... • Improve communication • Increase leadership and team effectiveness • Recognize untapped potential in current team members • Build trust and stronger relationships
VALUES	**So you can...** effect change, drive transformation, and make a difference to your customers and business.
DREAMS	**Ultimately the intention is to help you...** create a culture where your team is bonded to a "fellowship of the ring" mission.

TINA - President and CEO of F500 Company	
Transformation	**Selling from Love Transformation Story**
PROBLEM	**Currently you...** need to evolve the culture and leadership for your team as new hires have bought into a culture that your leadership team is not role modelling.
GOAL	**You want to...** create cultural norms that evolve the way you lead so that you can be open and flexible to maintain pace in a fast, ever-changing digital marketplace.
YOUR DIFFERENCE	This team building workshop will help you.... • Improve communication • Increase leadership and team effectiveness • Recognize untapped potential in current team members • Build trust and stronger relationships
VALUES	**So you can...** focus on the customer and build strong collaboration within the organization.
DREAMS	**Ultimately the intention is to help you...** leverage the talent of a multi-generational leadership table; honor the legacy leadership style of the tried and true, while at the same time being open and receptive to the entrepreneurial leadership style of innovation and experimentation.

JEFF – Founder and CEO Tech Startup	
Transformation	**Selling from Love Transformation Story**
PROBLEM	**Currently you…** have a remote working, overworked team that has experienced quick growth in staff and there's a concern of decreasing engagement or worse, losing staff due to burnout or lack of physical proximity.
GOAL	**You want to…** reconnect and restore the team to stay healthy, work better together, and move forward on your business priorities effectively.
YOUR DIFFERENCE	This team building workshop will help you…. • Improve communication • Increase leadership and team effectiveness • Recognize untapped potential in current team members • Build trust and stronger relationships.
VALUES	**So you can…** stay true to your "start-up" culture while at the same time manage growth in a structure that doesn't infringe on company spirit, as you need to be agile, nimble, and maintain pace in a fast and ever-changing marketplace.
DREAMS	**Ultimately the intention is…** to create a people culture program that supports the development of your people which focuses on onboarding, recruitment, and culture.

When using the Selling From Love Transformation Story, don't be a robot and read it word for word. Use the template as a foundation for your conversations and to help you connect with your client. You don't have to repeat their words exactly, but rather focus on the spirit of what they want.

My recommendation is that you use the questions in each of the selling from love transformations in your initial and ongoing client meetings and conversations. Discover what your client is struggling with most, what they want most, what is most important to them, and what a fulfilled life would be for them. Your Selling From Love Transformation Story is a reference point for you to reconnect with what is top of mind for your clients. Read the script prior to meeting with a client to help you focus on what is most important to them. You can download this template in the Sell From Love Workbook here www.sellfromlove.com/workbook.

CHAPTER EIGHT: SPEAK YOUR CLIENT'S LOVE LANGUAGE

EACH OF US has a preferred way to think, connect, and take action. For instance, you may be someone who needs to think through an idea before you act, or you may be the type of person who takes action first and thinks about it afterwards. Or perhaps you're quick on your feet to respond, or you're someone who needs to pause, go inwards, and reply with less speed and more thought. You may be someone who likes to ask many questions before making a decision or someone who relies on your level of excitement and enthusiasm as a deciding factor.

Just like you, your clients think, connect, and take action in their unique way. This may be different and often it is different from yours. If you don't know how your client communicates, you may assume your client does not want your service because they're asking so many questions, which you perceive more as distrust rather than genuine interest. Perhaps they don't say a word during your meeting and are quiet, but you're jumping out of your seat with excitement, sharing all the details of your latest service that you know will help, and now you think they're bored and disinterested.

What you may be missing is that it's not that they're disinterested or bored or interrogating you—they are interested, excited, and eager to learn more. The thing is, they speak a different love language than you may recognize. When selling from love, you want to honor who you are and the love language you prefer to communicate in. You can communicate in any of the five selling from love languages; however, you will lean more to one or two preferred styles. The beauty is that selling from love invites you to inquire and discover and honor your client's love language by choosing to make their language your preferred communication style when engaging with them.

Sell From Love Languages in Action

I remember a client back when I was a financial adviser. Let's call him Jack. Jack had a few million dollars invested in his portfolio and every month he'd come in demanding the best rates and at the lowest cost on his investments.

He was direct, assertive, and insistent. He knew exactly what he wanted and there was no changing his mind. He didn't convey much emotion and was far from warm.

My personal experience of him was that he was intimidating, aggressive and, at times, downright terrifying. The one day each month he'd visit my office was a wash. I was so stressed before he came in that I couldn't get anything done and would stir in my seat, spending the hours before he arrived reviewing his portfolio and calling the treasury and bond desk to reserve the best rates we had available for him. Then, the meeting would entail his detailing how unhappy he was with the rates being offered and threatening to take his money elsewhere. By the end of the meeting I felt like a puppy with my tail caught between my legs, taking orders and saying "yes sir".

He left with ego intact. I, on the other hand, felt figuratively as if I were on the floor and torn to shreds.

It wasn't until I understood that this was his modus operandi that I stopped agonizing over every word I said and ruining a good day because I had an upcoming meeting with Jack. He was a direct, know-what-I-want-and-I-will-tell-you kind of client. I learned these three lessons from Jack:

1. I stopped taking his communication style as a personal attack.

2. I understood that how he responded said more about him than me.

3. If I connected and communicated in his love language everything would change.

And it did. One day I decided not to allow fear to ruin my day and experience with this client. I was going to meet Jack with the same tone, directness, and assertiveness he demonstrated. I was no longer going to back down and fret if he threatened to take his investments elsewhere. I was going to offer our best rates with no further negotiation or knee-trembling fear. It was going to be said and that was the bottom line, even if that meant he'd take his investments elsewhere. Selling from fear was not going to dominate.

With my shoulders back, standing tall, I greeted Jack with a firm handshake as he entered my office. We exchanged quick pleasantries and he instantly moved to our business at hand, ready to take charge and bark his orders. I paused, took a deep breath, and mentally reminded myself to meet him where he was, to be his mirror, not his puppet. Instead of replying with a yes, let me call the bond desk to see if I can squeeze another 0.10% on top of the best rate I have already reserved, I replied "Jack, this is the best rate we can do for you. Nothing more." My voice was steady, calm, and certain. He believed me and didn't haggle. He took my word as I spoke to him in his love language.

Things did change for Jack and me. He did not take his investments elsewhere. My direct style of communication was well received. It was what he wanted all along and what our client-adviser relationship needed. He needed me to speak his love language in order to trust, respect, and have loyalty toward our business partnership. I no longer feared my meetings with Jack. I actually looked forward to them and appreciated working with a client who was so direct. It was refreshing. It also helped Jack to trust me more. Prior to this, he was not interested in any ideas or investment suggestions I had. After this he was more open and willing to hear and opt for other options which earned him better rates of return.

It's important to speak your clients' love language so that you can better understand and know who they are and what they need. It will help you strengthen your empathy muscles and create a stronger bond and foundation of trust with your client. Learning to speak their love language helps you not to take it personally if they don't respond in the way you thought they would. You learn not to assume that everyone communicates, connects, and makes decisions as you do.

The Five Selling from Love Languages

There are five selling from love languages. Each of them is distinct with its own unique characteristics and personality. Your client will use one or two of these love languages to communicate, connect, process information, brainstorm ideas, make a decision, and take action. It's through your conversations, meetings, and interactions that you have an opportunity to identify which of these love languages your client uses most. The five Sell from Love Languages are:

1. Language of Certainty

2. Language of Connection

3. Language of Confidence

4. Language of Consequence

5. Language of Change

Let's do a deeper dive into each of the sell from love languages so you can learn more about them. As you read the descriptions of each of the love languages, think about yourself. In what ways does this love language sound like you? In what way does it not sound like you? Consider your clients: does a particular love language remind you of one of your clients? I find it helpful to put names behind these love languages. By recalling someone who speaks this language, it'll make it easier for you to reference and discern whether the client you're meeting in the moment speaks more or less like the person to whom you've assigned a love language. For instance, in Chapter 7 you met Matt, Tina, and Jeff. Matt speaks the language of Change, Tina the language of Certainty, and Jeff the language of Confidence. When I meet a new client, I compare them to the characteristics that Matt, Tina, and Jeff demonstrate. It's easier to recall a client than the individual details of each of the love languages. This is how you'll quickly and easily learn each of the love language qualities. Use a client you know well and let them be the example you compare your clients to in each of the love language categories. Now let's learn more about them.

Language of Certainty

The language of Certainty depends on the tried and true to determine the best next step. These clients rely on facts, data, and past performance to make decisions. They prefer things to be organized in a process and always to have a plan. Those who speak the language of Certainty endeavour to build loyal relationships. Before moving forward, they want to feel secure and tend to rely on options that will give them stability and will feel familiar. People would describe them as consistent, conventional, emotionally stable, practical, and reliable.

Language of Connection

The language of Connection has a primary objective to build strong relationships. People who speak this language use their emotions to connect with others. They don't hold back their feelings; they openly express them. They tend to rely on their intuition and gut to make decisions. They often have a diverse social network and feel a sense of social responsibility. Those who speak the language of Connection easily express their excitement and enthusiasm. People would describe them as warm, passionate, empathetic, outgoing, and friendly.

Language of Confidence

The language of Confidence is always looking to take action and move forward. These clients naturally take ownership and the lead. They make their own decisions and are goal-oriented and outcome-focused. Those who speak the language of Confidence have a strong sense of self-belief and confidence. People would describe them as self-assured, determined, results-oriented, direct, and ambitious leaders.

Can you guess the love language for my client Jack? He led with the language of Confidence. His take-charge, direct, and assertive communication style demonstrated that clearly. He didn't express much emotion; often I couldn't tell what he was thinking unless he told me. He had a good poker face, hence I concluded that the language of Connection wasn't his highest suit. He was risk-averse; most of his investments were in bonds and treasury products instead of stocks and mutual funds. He didn't take any risk with his money. This was a clear indication that his complementary language was Certainty and not Change.

Language of Consequence

The language of Consequence is forward-looking—not from a visionary perspective; rather, these clients are looking to mitigate negative consequences. They are proactive and seek to avoid bad things from happening to good people. They will look under every rock to ensure something won't go wrong. You get brownie points when you do this on their behalf. Those who speak the language of Consequence are risk-averse and cautious, wanting all their I's dotted and T's crossed. People would describe them as detail-oriented, diligent, proactive, restrained, and organized.

Language of Change

The language of Change prefers autonomy and variety. These clients like to be challenged and to solve something in a new and innovative way. Instead of opting for the tried and true, they prefer to brainstorm new ways of solving old problems. Those who speak the language of Change are comfortable with ambiguity and embrace change and the new. People would describe them as spontaneous, adaptable, creative, independent, and bold.

The Do's and Don't's When Communicating with Each Sell from Love Language

You want to make a good impression, create a connection, and build a long-lasting relationship with your client. Identifying how your client prefers to communicate, connect, and take action are foundational when you sell from love. Learning how to speak in your client's language is not only about making it easier for you to sell your services. When you communicate in your client's language, you help them get what they most want faster, and with more clarity and ease. You've removed the potential for communication to be lost in translation which often stops a client from calling you back or stops you following up because you've assumed they're not interested.

The following charts provide you with the five do's and five don't's for each of the selling from love languages. This will give you practical, conversational, and relationship-building techniques you need to meet your clients where they are.

Language of Certainty	
Communication Do's	• Do use client testimonials, case studies and client examples that demonstrate where your product, service, or expertise provided value and delivered success.
	• Do describe the process and a clear path outlining steps that need to be taken.
	• Do use data, facts, and information to illustrate the benefits and past performance of your solution.
	• Do define how your offer will bring more stability, calm, and comfort to their business or life.
	• Do send materials your client can review in advance of meetings, to provide context and information, as well as after the meeting be sure to follow-up, as they will have more questions.

Communication Don'ts	• Don't expect your client to say yes instantly to your new and out-of-this-world offer. They need to see a track record and know it works. • Don't seek to connect with them at an emotional, heart-centric level. Their preference is to engage and interact at an intellectual, head-centric level. • Don't be disappointed if your client doesn't mirror your excitement and enthusiasm. Their outward emotional expression is not a sign of lack of interest or engagement. • Don't be intimidated if your client asks a lot of questions or is quiet during meetings. They are going inwards thinking and processing. • Don't attempt to facilitate a big, bold, and outside-the-box change for your client. They rely on the tried and true, steady and stable, with an incremental rather than breakthrough approach.

The best value you can provide: When your clients speak the language of Certainty, they can become paralyzed in indecision. They are continually looking for more information, data, and facts to give them comfort and safety in making a decision. This is especially true when venturing into new territory, be it purchasing something they've never purchased before or working with someone new.

When selling from love, the best value you can offer your client is to provide them with just the right amount of information, insights, facts, and data to satisfy the protector in them. You're helping them make the safest, most logical and reliable decision that will help them solve their problems, achieve their goals, honor a need, or fulfill a dream.

Using the selling from love language of Certainty, you're giving your clients comfort and peace of mind to move forward.

Language of Connection	
Communication Do's	• Do use warmth, emotions, and physical presence to connect and communicate with your client. • Do tell stories and use metaphors to describe the outcome your client can expect as a result of working with you. • Do invite your clients to visualize and describe what they are feeling about their current state and how they would feel in their future dream state. • Do demonstrate how your solution will create more connection, build stronger relationships, and add value to their personal and social network. • Do show your personal belief, excitement, and enthusiasm towards the solution you're offering and at the opportunity to work with them.

Communication Don'ts	• Don't use lots of logic and data, to convince, only enough to inform and satisfy their rational brain that their emotional brain is making the best decision.
	• Don't be reserved or detached, with your emotions. Your client is fueled by emotion and engages with feelings expressed in the meeting.
	• Don't be overly absorbed in analyzing the details of the problem and issue. Getting into the weeds doesn't energize or excite your client.
	• Don't narrow your conversation to focus only on the business at hand. Your client wants to share everything with you, be it personal, family, hobbies or favorite pastimes.
	• Don't focus on the practical and pragmatic features and benefits your solution delivers.

The best value you can provide: When your client speaks the language of Connection, they can get overwhelmed by their own emotions. These emotions can make it difficult for them to make a decision. One moment they are feeling excited to work with you or buy your service. Moments later, they are flooded with fear and doubt because of the significant investment or cost they are making and are stalled in indecision.

When selling from love, the best value you can offer your client is to remind them of what life will look like and feel like when they solve their problems, achieve their goals, honor a need, or fulfill their dreams. You're inviting them to connect to the feelings they will have, the relationships they will build, and the connections they will have when they achieve the desired future state they are wanting.

Using the selling from love language of Connection you're giving your clients an experience of emotion and relationship. They can then move forward, feeling this joy.

Language of Confidence	
Communication Do's	• Do empower your clients to take the lead and respect their role and desire to make the final decision. • Do focus on the big picture, not the details, and highlight the tangible result your product or service will deliver. • Do define how your solution will help them achieve results, lead better, and enhance the way others perceive them. • Do communicate clearly and concisely with an agenda, key objectives, and outcomes for your client meeting. • Do present a clear call to action with options on which your client can confidently make the final call and decision.

Communication Don'ts	• Don't use soft, fuzzy, tentative language when communicating. Be clear, direct, and focus on results.
	• Don't commandeer or overstep your client's authority. Let them sit in the driver's seat as you lead by being the trusted partner and confident guide.
	• Don't be intimated by their leadership and power.
	• Don't let your client over-bear or over-run your meetings with demands and unrealistic requests. Bring balance by being stable in your emotions and clear on your intentions.
	• Don't be over-sensitive or send signals that you are inefficient or incompetent. Instead focus on demonstrating that they can depend on you to achieve their goals, provide candid feedback, and validate their direction.

The best value you can provide: When your client speaks the language of Confidence, they can get in their own way by turning their assertive, action-oriented leadership style into an aggressive, my-way-or-the-highway authoritarianism. This may get the job done, but they may be the only one standing on top of the mountain. Because of their demanding nature and focus on getting results, they run the risk of losing relationships while trying to get to their destination.

When selling from love, the best value you can offer your client is to give them a safe and confidential place to be vulnerable. Often, they push down their emotions, holding back from expressing their fears, uncertainties, and doubts. This is a part of them they don't show to anyone, or to only a few trusted people. You're helping them by giving them a place to express these emotions.

Selling from the love language of Confidence, you're giving your clients clarity and control to lead, take action, or make decisions.

Language of Consequence	
Communication Do's	• Do set a clear and detailed timetable on what they can expect and by when, and make sure you stick to them. • Do know that the devil is in the detail. Your client will lean on order and regulation. They want to follow the rules. • Do address your client's objections in advance, before they even ask. • Do highlight the negative consequence they will avoid or prevent if they decide to work with you. • Do offer ideas and suggestions on how your client can mitigate any negative outcome.
Communication Don'ts	• Don't make mistakes, or at least do your best to avoid them. Your client relies on accuracy and order. • Don't miss a deadline. If you do, be proactive and let your client know in advance you won't be delivering their request in the committed timeframe. • Don't avoid or hide the truth, especially when things don't go as planned. • Don't forget or go light on the details. Always keep them in the loop because the more they know the more confidence they have. • Don't gloss over potential risks or what may go wrong. They want to know them and have a plan to address them.

The best value you can provide: When your client speaks the language of Consequence, they want to avoid problems and challenges. However, this avoidance can create more problems for them as they get caught up in all the details, micro-managing to have more control. Striving to create the perfect solution holds them back from having any solution at all. They don't want to make a mistake and fear getting it wrong so much that they don't decide at all. Not making a decision is a decision too.

When selling from love, the best value you can offer your client is to be proactive and provide them with a precise, detailed analysis of what may not go as planned and how it can be addressed. They are cautious, risk-averse, and put careful thought in before making a decision. Craft a pro-con list and give them time to contemplate their options. You're helping them make accurate, ideal, and high-quality decisions that will help them solve their problems, achieve their goals, honor a need, or fulfill a dream.

Using the selling from love language of Consequence, you're giving your clients a defensive position and an objective plan to move forward.

Love Language of Change	
Communication Do's	• Do make time in your meeting to let your client brainstorm ideas and next steps, and to collect and edit the best ones. • Do give your clients autonomy to come up with their own solutions and decision-making to solve their problems or achieve their goals. • Do present products, services, and solutions that are new, fresh, and cutting-edge to your client. • Do provide a sounding board for your clients to validate their ideas and next steps. • Do focus your conversation on the change and new possibility that taking this next step will create for them.
Communication Don'ts	• Don't rely on solving their problems with past tried and true methods. They prefer trying something new that hasn't been done before. • Don't limit ideas, possibilities, or ways to solve their problems or achieve their goals with one solution. They prefer variety and a chance to create their own custom solution. • Don't hold to a structured agenda during your client meetings. You can have an outline, but always remember to give lots of freedom in the frame. • Don't move to action or decision-making too early. Be sure to give your client time to flush out all possible ideas and solutions. • Don't demand a rigid process or meticulous plan. Be flexible, fluid, and make room for your client to shift direction.

The best value you can provide: When your client speaks the language of Change, they can get overpowered with too many ideas, action items, and solutions. This in turn leads them to try to do everything, leading to nothing changing. They are continually looking for the next big idea or change, which can hold them back from deciding on doing one thing and making something big happen in that area.

When selling from love, the best value you can offer your clients is to provide them a place to explore, brainstorm, and dream of big ideas and new possibilities as they consider how to solve their problems, achieve their goals, honor a need, or fulfill a dream.

Using the selling from love language of Change, you're giving your clients a place to imagine the ideal and to create new ways of solving old problems.

Determining Your Client's Sell From Love Language.

Now you may be asking yourself: how do you figure out which sell from love language your client speaks? Remember, your clients speak each language; however, they will focus on one or two more than the others. You don't want to put your client in a box with a label as it can limit how you share your offers or can impede your relationship. Your client is a dynamic human. You want to be open-minded and hold a broad view of which language is being spoken at any given time. Context, circumstance, and your client's life situation will impact their language preference.

For example, a client receives a promotion that requires her family to move neighborhoods and buy a new home. Working with her real-estate agent, she speaks the language of Change and Confidence. She's been talking about making a move for some time and this promotion was the perfect catalyst. Now let's take the same family and instead of a promotion that would require a change in neighborhoods, they need to move overseas to a new country. Even though they were looking for some change, the magnitude of this change has them speaking the language of Certainty and Confidence..

They want to feel safe, have comfort, and be assured in making this new home purchase.

So how do you figure out which language your client is speaking? You lean on what you've already learned in Chapter 5; you use your selling from love skills. By doing your homework, listening with intent, being present to what your client is saying and not saying, remaining quiet in the moments of pause and asking open, curious, wonder-filled questions, you will discover your client's language.

As you prepare, jot down some questions to ask your client about decisions they've made in the past. What was important when they made that decision? What were some of the things they considered? For instance, if the client made a big move in the past, invite them to tell you more about what criteria they used to make the big move.

Here are a few questions you can sprinkle into your client conversations to pick up on which language is their preference at this moment for this given situation:

- What is holding you back from making a decision?

- What do you need to move forward? What else?

- What is most important to you right now? Why is that important to you? By having/attaining this, what would it give you?

- What would the next ideal step be for you?

- What could bring you more comfort and ease right now?

Now if you're finding it difficult to figure out your client's preferred language or it's still too early in your relationship to define it, here's a language priority list. This priority list is based on how our human brain is designed. First, you use the love language of Certainty to satisfy your client's lizard brain, next you use Connection to fulfill the emotional left brain, and finally you use Consequence to meet the needs of the logical and rational right brain. Here is more detail on your language priority list:

Priority 1: Using the language of Certainty enables you to create safety, reliability, and credibility with your client. You build rapport and a foundation of trust that clients learn they can depend on. They have comfort in knowing the outcomes to expect, based on past results or your track record.

Priority 2: Next, you want to move from establishing rapport to building a relationship using the language of Connection. This is where you bring more emotion and personal stories, and you encourage your clients to embody the feelings they would have after they experience the transformation they are after.

Priority 3: You've established rapport with Certainty, built a relationship with Connection, and now you want to help your clients rationalize their decisions using the love language of Consequence. They want to know that what they want is what they'll get, with no obstacles or problems standing in the way. They need to make logical sense of their emotional desire.

You're helping your clients make a decision and move forward to experience the transformation they are seeking. When selling from love, your intentions are to serve, have their best interests at heart first and foremost, and communicate in a way that will help them hear that the solution you are recommending will help them get there. Selling from love means that you do this with integrity and seek to deepen your empathy skills by not only putting yourself in your client's shoes, but by speaking their love language too.

RECAP

Let's review before we move on:

In Part Two – Love Your Client, we talked about how important it is for you to love your client in order to sell from love. There are four ways in which you have an opportunity to demonstrate this love so that your client knows you genuinely care, understand, and want to help them.

First, it's through your sell from love skills of preparation, deep listening, asking open and wonder-filled questions, and allowing for silence and pause in your conversation. It's through these skills you show your true intentions by giving your clients space and an active, interested listening ear as they share their stories and their needs.

Second, you demonstrate this love by moving your attention away from what's in it for you to what's in it for them. By putting yourself in their shoes, using empathy to see the world from their eyes, your clients walk away with an inner peace, knowing they were heard and understood.

Third, you learned how to reframe what you're selling. It's not about the product, service, or expertise you bring. That's the transaction. Rather, what you're really selling is the transformation. It's who your client gets to be, what they get to have, and what they can do because they decided to say yes to working with you.

Finally, the last piece you discovered was about the five sell from love languages. We speak all five of these languages. However, we tend to lean toward one or two more often. Your client may be speaking a different language from you and things may be getting lost in translation. In the past it may have cost you an opportunity, but now you have the tools to communicate, connect, and clearly articulate your message in the sell from love language your client prefers most.

We're off to Part 3: Love Your Offer, the third and final stage to sell from love. Your offer is what brings you and your client together, it's what brings purpose and meaning to your work and allows you to experience all the rewards and benefits that come when you sell from love. This is the cherry on top. I can't wait to dig in with you. Let's get started.

PART THREE:

—

LOVE YOUR OFFER

CHAPTER NINE:
FALL IN LOVE WITH YOUR OFFER

—

"You've got to find what you love. And that is as true for your work as it is for your lovers. Your work is going to fill a large part of your life, and the only way to be truly satisfied is to do what you believe is great work."

Steve Jobs

FOR A SALE to happen, there has to be an offer. Your offer is what you're selling, the product, service, or expertise you are offering to your client. If you had nothing to offer, there could be no sale. Your offer opens the door for you to connect, engage, and create change for your client.

Love is an integral part of your offer. Yes, this is true even when selling a mortgage, dental supplies, or project-management software. This means that you love the idea, product, service, or expertise you're offering to your client. Look at it this way: if you don't love it, how could you expect your client to? You need to love it and it's through this love that you'll attract, engage, and build a relationship with your client. When you love your offer, selling from fear cannot hold you back from sharing it with others, especially when it comes to marketing your offers, which we'll talk about in Chapters 10 and 11.

But, of course, you may not always love your offer. You may not love it because

- You don't believe or have confidence in your product, service, or solution and you don't believe that it will deliver on its promise.

- You are not passionate or excited about selling your product, service, or solution.

- The product, service, or solution you're selling doesn't align to your personal values or beliefs.

Fair enough. Most of us have been there. You may be asking yourself: *can you sell from love, even if you don't love your offer?* The short answer is no. The longer answer is the rest of this chapter.

Don't take not loving or believing in what you sell as a bad thing or think you have to quit or twist yourself into knots to use this process. Consider it simply a message telling you something is amiss.

Not loving your offer could be informing you that you have something to learn about the product or service you are providing. You're not loving it because you don't fully understand its value, the impact it delivers, or you don't yet grasp and appreciate the magnitude of the transformation your clients realize as a result of your offer. You're being invited to deepen the love you have for the product you are selling.

Alternatively, it could be an indication that it's time to expand the love you have for your offer. Once a upon a time, you were overjoyed and fueled with passion to sell your service. But now it feels passé, a been-there-done-that kind of situation. To fall back in love may mean expanding and broadening to whom you are providing your services. You're being called to step up to your next level of impact, to touch more clients, or reach out to a different kind of client than you've worked with in the past.

Finally, not loving your offer may mean it's time for a change. The season of selling from love for this particular service or your current expertise level has come to an end. It's time to spring into something new and fresh.

When you sell from love you've got an opportunity at hand, an opportunity to learn, grow, and evolve. When you don't love your offer, it's an indication that you're at risk of moving away from love and selling from fear. Know that when you do the work to fall in love with your idea or expertise, there's a transformation available not only for your clients, but for you as well.

It's Your Responsibility to Learn How to Fall in Love with Your Offer

The good news? Simply having the *intention* or desire to fall in love with what you are selling will get you on your way. By taking responsibility *and* taking action to find love in your offer, you will be in better shape to use the process in this book to love your clients and yourself, and make more sales. I'll explain more, but first meet Jenny, Jim, and Clara, three people who did not love what they were selling.

Jenny had made the leap from the corporate world of human resources to opening her own HR consulting firm. Even though she's doing the exact same work, she's doing it as an entrepreneur for several different clients versus one employer. Jenny's not only in charge of HR programs but, as an entrepreneur, she's head of finance, sales and marketing, and administration. The additional responsibility has thrown her completely out of her comfort zone. Jenny is doubting her abilities, questioning her value, and wondering if her company can deliver on its promises. Jenny's confidence has waned and she's falling out of love with her HR programs and why she started her company in the first place.

Jim is a financial adviser who specializes in investment planning for busy corporate professionals. He's been doing this work for twenty years and, lately, he feels like Bill Murray in *Groundhog Day*. His passion for doing portfolio reviews, the thrill of closing a new client, and his enthusiasm to share his knowledge with new advisers has faded. Jim misses the days when he loved Monday mornings and the burst of potential and eagerness he felt at the start of a month, quarter, and year.

And finally, meet Clara, a pharmaceutical sales rep. She started working for her company selling asthma medications. This was something near and dear to her heart because her eldest child suffered from asthma. But Clara's company is shifting directions and instead of selling asthma medicine, they've moved her to their anti-anxiety drug department. It's not that she doesn't believe in these medicines, it's that she all too often sees them being over-prescribed before alternatives such as therapy, meditation, and nutrition are scoped out or included. It's hard for her to sell something that doesn't align to her values and this is holding her back from loving it fully.

How Do Jenny, Jim, and Clara Find the love?

First, they need to be sure that they are separating out their fear of making an offer from *what* they're offering. Presenting your products, services, and expertise to your clients creates an ideal environment for fear to highjack your brain and your thinking. Selling from fear often shows up—ta da!—just when you're about to make your pitch or presentation. Suddenly you find yourself focused on the transactional element of what you're offering—what's in it for you—rather than on your client and the *transformation* your service will deliver.

When we lose sight of what our offer gives to others, we can lose our enthusiasm, energy, and confidence.

Three Ways to Fall in Love with Your Offer

It's your job to figure out how your product will serve, transform, and deliver on its promise to your client. There are three ways you can fall in love with your offer and reconnect to selling from love. First, you need to believe in your offer and the promise it will deliver to your clients. Second, you need to realize that your services are a vehicle for you to deliver on your purpose and to reconnect with that purpose once again. And finally, it's important to recognize that not only is your client receiving a transformation from what you are selling, so are you.

Now let's do a deeper dive into each of these areas.

Way Forward #1: Develop Belief in Your Offer

You need to believe in what you're selling. You need to believe that your expertise will add value and make a meaningful difference. You need to believe that it solves a problem, creates a transformation, and is of service to your client. When you believe in your offer, you create a magnetic energy that attracts ideal clients to your business. When you sell from this place, you genuinely believe that what you're offering will create a positive change in the lives you're affecting.

But how do you get there when you don't believe? Here are five things you can do to instill more belief in what you deliver to your clients:

1. <u>Set an intention.</u> Create an intention to fall in love with your offer even if you don't love it or are afraid to put it out there. Be willing to fall in love, even if there is no love there yet. Declaring the desire to love with an openness and curiosity to uncover the value your offer delivers is the best place to start. In Chapter 4 you learned about the positive-power primers. This is a great way to set an intention. Tell yourself:

   - I am willing to love (insert the name of your product, service, or expertise).

   - I choose to love (insert the name of your product, service, or expertise).

   - I believe I can love (insert the name of your product, service, or expertise).

   - I love (insert the name of your product, service, or expertise).

2. <u>Identify what's on your edge:</u> Do the comfort to courage zone activity from Chapter 3 and identify where your offer lands. Is it in your comfort zone? On the edge? In your courage zone? Brainstorm options and actions you can take to add more comfort to your offer. It could be focusing your product or service on clients with whom you have strong relationships, conducting a pilot or hosting a focus group to get feedback directly from your clients. Be sure to take

action, while giving your offer a "safe" place for you to learn how to fall in love with it.

3. <u>Focus on low-hanging fruit</u>: Humans prefer the path of least resistance. This goes for you as well as your clients. Fear of rejection or fear of failure may be getting in the way of loving your service. This fear generates resistance, giving you valid reasons why you should not sell or love your offer. To circumvent this, make it easier on yourself by placing your products, services, and expertise in front of clients you're most comfortable with. These are your low-hanging fruit clients. They are people you believe would get the most out of your solution, and if you failed miserably in front of them it wouldn't feel like the end of the world.

4. <u>Present and propose your offer</u>: Knowledge without action is simply information; knowledge *with* action leads to transformation. You need to put your idea, product or service into the hands of your clients. When you present them, you discover the right words to use. During client conversations you learn what words, questions, and stories connect. You learn your client's objections and whether anything needs to change about how you're making the offer. Each time you present to a potential client you learn, and you fall in love even more. Over time you get better and one day you're so good that you sell from only love, with ease and flow.

5. <u>Collect feedback, stories and testimonials from your clients</u>: Your clients can help you fall in love with your offer. Gathering their feedback, personal experiences, and results they received from working with you will not only validate your offer but dramatically increase your ability to love it. My favorite questions to ask are:

- What was most useful and valuable to you?

- What are the three things you're taking away?

- What is different now that we've worked together?

- What tangible result or impact could you attribute to our working together?

Enjoy the positive, affirming feedback. Use it to fall in love with your offers and, with your clients' permission, share their stories with prospective clients to make it easier for them to fall in love with your offer too.

Our HR entrepreneur, Jenny, set an intention to fall in love with her HR programs. By stating a clear desire, she put herself on the path to selling from love, even though she's not feeling the love right now. Because there's so much change, learning, and growth occurring for her with starting a new business, Jenny's completely beyond her comfort zone. Acknowledging this helps her see it's not that she doesn't believe in her HR programs, it's that she's lacking the know-how and confidence in her business systems and processes. As a result, she decides to focus her business development activities on her network that already knows, likes, and trusts her. She'll work on broadening her market presence once her team, systems, and business processes are in place and when she feels assured in her business.

Jenny knows she needs to build her business and the only way to do that is by putting out proposals. Even though they're not all landing in big contracts, she's learning how to respond to client's queries and objections in the moment and addressing their concerns with more ease. After five proposal presentations and one brand-new client, she's feeling more confident in her programs. One of her most important clients referred another client to her and Jenny received a rave review from the new client. The culmination of Jenny's setting an intention to love her HR programs, taking steps that were on the edge of her comfort zone, and putting proposals out to clients who know, like, and trust her helped fuel her belief that she can deliver on her client's promise, even though she's still learning the ropes of running a business. Step by step, by taking incremental action, Jenny has fallen in love with her offer.

Way Forward #2: Revisit and Expand the Meaning of Your Work

In his book *Go Put Your Strengths to Work*, Marcus Buckingham shares that most people are actually in their ideal jobs.[1] However, over time, the happiness, fulfillment, and love they once felt fades. Most people start thinking that they're in the wrong job or need to change careers completely. But what if that isn't the case? Based on a nationally representative workforce, Marcus discovered what most people want is not to change jobs; instead, they want to increase the responsibility they have in their jobs or they're looking to dive deeper into a specialized subset of their work.

Let's look at Jim and explore what options are available to help him reconnect with the love he once had for his work and what he sells.

1. **Expand Your Impact**: Jim has twenty years of knowledge and experience as a financial adviser. This information and insight can be used to educate and enlighten colleagues, clients, and industry professionals. Jim could start writing articles on LinkedIn to share how to run an effective and successful practice or he could launch a podcast to mentor others. He could develop a mastermind for new financial planners. Jim could bring in new financial advisers to his team, giving him a chance to coach and mentor while freeing up time so he could speak at conferences and change up his routine.

2. **Niche Your Impact**: Currently Jim provides investment planning to corporate professionals. However, over the past few years he's grown more interested in what entrepreneurs are up to, especially start-ups working to solve deeply entrenched social and environmental problems. He loves reading about the latest start-up trends in *Entrepreneur* and *Fast Company* magazines. He really enjoys the innovative and pioneering spirit entrepreneurs bring to big problems. One way Jim could bring back more love to his work is by refining who he serves and how he serves them. Instead of investment planning for corporate professionals, he could offer cash-flow planning for start-ups. Or in lieu of leaving the industry entirely, he could focus on a niche or specialized subset of his work he can fall back in love with. Jim has a wealth of knowledge that is invaluable to colleagues, clients, and his industry. Falling out of love doesn't mean he needs to leave his job; all it means is that that he has an opportunity to find different ways to fall back in love with it. The same goes for you, especially if you're selling something you once loved. Is there a

way for you to love it once again by expanding or changing who you reach, who you serve, or how you deliver your products or services?

Way Forward #3: Put Your Attention on the Transformation

In Chapter 7: "Love the Transformation, Not Only the Transaction", we examined how your offer is the vehicle you use to facilitate a transformation for your clients. It's the thing you use to help your client solve a problem, achieve a goal, honor a need, or fulfill a dream. Shifting your attention off the thing you're selling—and what it gets you—and onto the impact it delivers opens the door to reconnect back to love. Remember Clara, our pharmaceutical sales rep who wasn't loving the change from selling asthma medication to anti-anxiety medication? For Clara, rather than putting the emphasis on the product she is selling, it's about directing her attention to the transformation patients experience after using anti-anxiety treatment. Even though she believes there are other ways to solve this problem, she can connect to the positive benefits people experience when using this medicine.

Clara is facilitating a transformation for her clients using this product, but her company and clients are also providing her with a transformation. Once a month, Clara receives a commission cheque. This money helps her pay her mortgage, put aside savings for her children's education, take self-improvement courses, and enjoy a yoga membership. Clara's work is helping her experience a transformation by providing a dream home to live in, fulfilling a goal to help her kids graduate debt-free, and satisfying her values of learning and self-care. Selling from love invites you to love your offer by appreciating not only the transformation you deliver to your clients but also the one you get to experience as a result.

I want to recognize that love for the transformation you're giving and the one you're receiving may not be enough for you to love your product or service. You don't have to force something that's not there. This may be the perfect time to revisit and evaluate where you are going in your work and what you most want. In Clara's case, she may decide to leave the company and go to one that is more aligned with her values or start something new in a completely different industry. As with any relationship, the season may come to an end. It's hard to stay in the same job because you're afraid to change. When we avoid this call for change because of fear, we will inevitably land back into selling from fear.

Falling in love with your product, service or expertise is not a one-and-done activity. It's a relationship. It needs work, commitment, intention, and open communication. The more you put in, the more you will get out of it. It takes time, effort, and energy, but the love and transformation you experience are well worth the investment. Go ahead, take the plunge, fall in love.

CHAPTER TEN:
MAKE IT EASY FOR CLIENTS TO FIND A WAY TO LOVE YOU

—

"The two most important things we can do are to allow ourselves to be seen AND to really see others. The greatest gift you can give a person is to see who she is and to reflect that back to her. When we help people to be who they want to be, to take back some of the permission they deny themselves, we are doing our best, most meaningful work."

Bernadette Jiwa

TO SELL YOU need to tell. People need to know that you are the perfect person to help them solve their problems, achieve their goals, honor their values, or fulfill their dreams. However, if you don't tell them, they'll never know. The whole notion of "build it and they will come" doesn't work. Never has.

You need to love your offer so much that you're willing to put yourself out there, out on a limb to tell them about it. Your clients need to know you built something specifically for them. You need to make it easy for clients to find and fall in love with you. Your clients need to know that you exist and that your expertise will change their life. They need to know why you love your offer, so they can love it too.

Presenting, promoting, and advocating for your offer creates an opportunity for you to bring your body of work to someone whom it will serve. It sets up the ideal environment for an invitation to happen, an invitation to make meaningful change, demonstrate value, and facilitate the transformation your clients have been waiting all this time to experience.

But it's never that easy, right? Standing up and giving a voice to your big ideas can be daunting and downright scary. You're putting yourself out there for rejection and disappointment, maybe even judgement and criticism—something your lizard brain isn't interested in and will do everything possible to avoid. Cue busy work, scrolling through Instagram on your phone, or whatever way you prefer to avoid putting yourself out there. And cue your inner critic and negative self-talk. You tell yourself you're not a salesperson, you're not a marketer, that you can't make the sales call because you suck.

Be the Voice of Your Offer; Make it Visible

In the past it may have cost you an opportunity, but now you have the tools to communicate, connect, and clearly articulate your message in the sell from love language your client prefers most. Asking for the business or closing the sale doesn't happen in the same way when you sell from love. Closing the sale is no longer an isolated event you must force yourself to do. It happens naturally and easily as the next logical step in your client's journey with you. Imagine this: what if instead of having to ask your clients to sign up to work with you, they're asking you? Don't be surprised if when you sell from love this becomes a normal and frequent experience. How cool is that?

When you sell from love, presenting and promoting your services comes with ease because you've done your homework:

- You've discovered and claimed your Brilliant Difference

- You've learned how to move from your comfort zone to your courage zone with self-love and self-care

- You've learned how to communicate what you offer in a language your clients understand

- You believe that your offer will make a positive change and impact on them

You may still be afraid to post your article on LinkedIn, make that call to a potential client, get on stage, or attend the networking event. However, when you sell from love you know you can handle whatever comes your way when you put yourself out there. You don't fear being crushed by failure or disappointment anymore.

Stop the Funnel

Traditional selling frameworks often use the term "sales funnel". I'm sure you've heard it a thousand times; maybe you've used it yourself. The sales funnel is the analogy for moving a client from initial contact to final sale. The stages involved in a sales funnel include awareness, interest, evaluation, intent, and then a sale. The useful thing about the funnel analogy is that the top is wider than the bottom. This is to remind you that you need many more people aware of you, your business, and your services at the start to have enough left at the end to close the sale. For instance, to get five sales you need a thousand people to be aware of you, a hundred interested, twenty evaluating, and ten with intent, to ultimately close five clients into one of your solutions.

That's all good, but what I don't like about the term funnel is it can make selling transactional. It focuses on the numbers and that can mean you forget there are real people with real problems you want to help. Sales funnels can get you so wrapped up in the tactics of selling that you forget to whom you're selling and why.

Sales funnels make it easy to visualize and manage the business of selling but can ultimately cost you sales because, just like a funnel, you're narrowing your focus. Selling from love values numbers, but not at the cost of losing sight of the human being behind the number. Selling from love is about moving a client through a transformation, not a transaction. You build a relationship with your clients. Selling from love puts you, your client, and your offer before profit and reminds you to lean on your Brilliant Difference, speak your client's love language, and believe in your offer, or you won't have any numbers to analyze in your spreadsheets.

Start Using a Megaphone

Instead of a sales funnel, consider selling from love as being more like a megaphone. A megaphone is used to amplify sound and direct voice. Its shape is similar but inverse to that of a funnel. The entry point is narrow with the exit wide and open, giving it the ability to magnify the sound coming out on the other side.

Think about selling from love from this perspective. You are not meant to work with everybody. Not everyone will value or get value from the products, services, and expertise you have to offer. There are only a select few. Therefore, the entry point to working with you is narrow. You're not funneling everyone through your sales process to find the few that will say yes to working with you. Instead you're being selective; you're discerning and choosing who gets to work with you and come in through your megaphone.

The end of a megaphone is open, wide, and amplifying. The voice coming out of this megaphone is the voice of your clients. You brought your Brilliant Difference, used your selling from love skills by listening with intent and open curiosity; your clients felt heard and understood. You connected using their preferred love language and took them away from having a transactional event to making a transformational shift in their business and life. They are walking away singing your praises, sharing your work, and spreading the love of your impact to their family, friends, colleagues, and anyone who will listen. You've unlocked the only marketing strategy that ever works: word of mouth. Stop the funnel from narrowing your voice; instead start using a megaphone to have other voices speak for you.

Helping People Move from Indifferent Outsider to Devoted Insider

Indifferent outsiders are people who don't know you, don't need you, or are not having the problem you solve for right now. They are also people who don't understand what you're selling or are too busy and distracted to notice what you're selling in the first place. They are also your ideal client: they have a problem you can solve, they are ready to say yes, and they are looking for you as much as you are looking for them. Indifferent outsiders are at the entry point of your sell from love megaphone.

As clients move from indifferent outsider, you're endeavoring to help them to become a devoted insider. A devoted insider is someone who buys from you repeatedly, and often; they are your most profitable clients. Profitable doesn't always mean they buy lots from you or buy your most expensive products and services. Devoted insiders reduce your acquisition costs because you don't have to invest tons of money in advertising, in Facebook or Google ads, and they're your best marketing strategy. Devoted insiders will talk you up to family, friends, and colleagues. A devoted insider is someone who will help you spread the word of your work as a result of having a sell from love experience with you.

So how do you turn an indifferent outsider and reap the benefits and value from a devoted insider? Stick with me here, read on, and you'll learn just how.

Make it Easy for Clients to Find You

Everyone starts with being an indifferent outsider. It's your responsibility to take action to inform and enlighten people about who you are, who you serve, and what you can help them with. At this stage you are casting a wide net with the intent to find your ideal clients and help them find you. This may be by posting an article on LinkedIn, attending a local networking event, or delivering a presentation at an industry event.

Once a link is made—from the sea of indifferent outsiders you notice your ideal client or your ideal client notices you—it's time to build trust and engagement. The aim is to motivate your ideal clients to engage or initiate some form of contact and connection with you.

When you've built enough trust and engaged your ideal client by demonstrating your Brilliant Difference, the transformation you deliver and the value they will receive, you've now moved to the next stage where you get the opportunity to create an invitation. This is the moment when either you offer your client a chance to work together or they're on the edge of their seat, with the words at the tip of their tongue waiting to ask you the same question.

When selling from love, you move through each of these stages to transition a client from indifferent outsider to a client you get to work with. Let's take a look at what you can do to move through each of these states with more confidence, ease, and success.

Stage 1: Inform and enlighten indifferent outsiders: This stage is all about creating brand awareness. This means you need to put yourself out there letting people know you exist, who you ideally work with, what problems you solve, what goals you help your clients achieve, and what you offer to help them do that. This is where an indifferent outsider becomes aware that you have something they want or that you can help them get what they want.

Ideal clients enter the sell from love process when you find ways to inform, educate, and enlighten them that you exist. You're letting them know you're the 'go to' person. Brand awareness activities keep you top of mind for when your client or someone they know is experiencing the problem you solve. You want your name to be the one they think of and the one they call. Increasing brand awareness happens through frequent, consistent touchpoints.

Sophie has been a successful financial adviser for the past two decades and two years ago her financial advisory firm was acquired by one of the big investment brokerage houses. Sophie's Brilliant Difference was her ability to build a successful practice and deliver innovative financial advice and solutions to clients without compromising integrity. In addition to that, her recent experience of working through a merger and acquisition added to her expertise.

Sophie is making a shift in her business. She wanted to deepen her Brilliant Difference and decided to move away from providing direct financial advice to her clients to offering merger and acquisition consulting to financial advisers who want to enter a M&A partnership. She's set up shop as a consultancy firm to help financial advisers and firms move through the process simply and successfully.

To inform and enlighten the market about her new consulting company, she broadcasted her new venture on a public relations newswire, reached out to colleagues in her network, and submitted applications to speak at conference events. Sophie was invited to be a speaker at an industry event which later turned into several interviews and feature articles with the top publications in her industry. Sophie is also posting articles on LinkedIn, so she remains top of mind to her network and that they know her Brilliant Difference is helping financial advisers and firms that are pursuing a merger and acquisition partnerships.

Sophie is generating awareness that her consulting firm has the knowledge, skills, and expertise to help financial advisers through the M&A process. By building a website, writing a blog, speaking on stages, and showing up at industry networking events, Sophie is making her Brilliant Difference visible. She is helping clients know that if they need coaching, guidance, or advice through a merger and acquisition, she's the perfect person to connect with.

You want to make it easy for ideal clients to find you. If you hide or don't make yourself visible you can't expect them to find you. Selling from love is not about pushing something on someone who doesn't need or want it. Selling from love is letting people know who you are, what you offer, who you serve, and the goals you can help them achieve. Your job is to inform and enlighten; do that and then we can move to the next step to build trust and engagement.

Ten activities you can implement to find ideal clients in the pool of indifferent outsiders

1. Write posts/articles on LinkedIn

2. Get a feature in industry publications

3. Host a seminar or presentation (online/offline)

4. Get interviewed on a relevant podcast

5. Attend networking events

6. Join a local business association or toastmasters

7. Facebook ads/Google ads

8. Public relations – broadcast on newswire

9. Media – be featured on local or national radio and TV

10. Build a website

Stage 2: Build trust and engagement with ideal clients: Now that they know you exist, you need to demonstrate that you are someone they can trust. It is as George Macdonald, in his book *The Marquis of Lossie*, said: "To be trusted is a greater compliment than being loved."[1] You do that by showing up consistently and giving through your Brilliant Difference with no strings attached. When you give like this, you fill up your future client's confidence bucket. They come to see you as a trusted adviser. You build rapport and reliability, and you plant the seeds of a strong relationship. Secondly, when it comes time to invite a client to work with you, when you've already overdelivered on value, you've also filled up your confidence bucket. You know you've earned the right to ask for their business.

Robert Cialdini talks about the six key factors to influence and persuasion in his book *Influence*[2]. In the law of reciprocity, he states: "If you do something nice for me, I'll do something nice for you. I feel obligated to reciprocate."

Think of a server in a restaurant who's gone above and beyond for you and your guests. When the bill comes you feel more inclined to hit the higher tip button instead of the customary button. Or let's say you're walking through the grocery store and the clerk is offering you a free perogi sample. Even though you weren't planning on buying any, you take one to try and then buy a package to take home. You took a sample and now you feel inclined to buy the whole package. This is the law of reciprocity in effect. When you sell from love, you not only receive the benefits from this law, you can increase them because you're overdelivering from a place of love.

Best-selling author and American psychologist Adam Grant, in his book *Give and Take*, says "Every time we interact with another person at work, we have a choice to make: do we try to claim as much value as we can, or contribute value without worrying about what we receive in return?" [3] When you give, you give with the intention to help and serve, rather than to get something. Giving to get is not selling from love. Giving to get is selling from fear. When you sell from love, you let your clients know you have their best interests at heart. You're providing advice, guidance, and resources to help your clients make the right decisions. You do this even before they've bought from you.

Three Ways to Build Trust and Engagement

There are three ways you can demonstrate value to build trust and engagement with ideal clients. First, you can educate your ideal client through content by sharing information with them through seminars, blogs, or research papers. Second, you can help your clients by making life easier for them by connecting them with people in your network when they're in a pinch or need a source or a recommendation. Finally, you can help ideal clients strengthen belief and trust in you every time you suggest an idea, insight, or resource that will directly make a positive contribution to their business or life.

Steve is a commercial banker and many of his clients are doctors and professionals who work in the medical arena. He's been working with his clients for two years and is looking to deepen and strengthen his relationship with them. His goals are to be his clients' primary banker and build a strong enough relationship with them that they'd refer people in their network to him for their banking needs. Let's see how Steve implements these top three giving strategies.

#1 Overdeliver Value through Content: Steve hosted a seminar to educate his clients on succession planning. Many of his clients were experienced doctors who had built up a significant practice of patients and wealth. They have a community of patients to consider when they move to the next stage of their life, and tax implications too. Steve wants his clients to plan, know what is waiting for them, and know what they need to do today to make the retirement process seamless.

#2 Overdeliver Value through Connection: Steve partnered with succession planning experts including an accountant, a lawyer, a business appraiser, a life coach, and a doctor who had recently retired. Steve's seminar wasn't about his products and services, it was to educate his clients about the entire succession process, everything they needed to succeed. He invited people he trusted so that his clients wouldn't need to search for the best expert information.

#3 Overdeliver Value through Contribution: Steve and his panel of experts each offered a personal consultation after the seminar. There was no upsell, no pressure to hire anyone. Each colleague freely offered his or her best advice, ideas, and insights to each attendee. Steve was making sure to go the extra mile to save his clients time and to help them make more money to contribute to their happiness, success, and fulfillment.

Overdelivering on value, with no strings attached, really works. It's the only way I know how to succeed. It has always worked for me in my twenty-five-year career in sales. There have been times when I've gotten stuck in the giving to get, selling from fear model and failed miserably or didn't receive as much as I expected. That's because I placed expectation on the giving and the performance pressure made the giving falter.

Recall in Chapter 1 when I took that Fascinate® personality test? At the time I was in a corporate role as an HR business partner. I had taken this test and, because it helped me so much, I knew it would help the team I was working with. I was in HR, not learning and development. I had never presented or facilitated a workshop in my life. But I felt compelled to help the leaders I was supporting and teams I was working with. I met with the executives and proposed to host a workshop for only the women of their department. One of their top agenda items was to increase the presence of women leaders in their area.

In my proposal presentation I emphasized how this workshop would increase confidence, improve female presence at the leadership table, and help the company meet their diversity and inclusion goals. It was the fastest pitch I had ever delivered. I attribute much of the success to selling from love and using the selling from love languages. They not only said they wanted the workshop for the women of their department, they wanted me to deliver it to their entire team of 350 employees. I can tell you, this was another holy crap, what have I gotten myself into, beyond courage zone moment!

The essence of this proposal came from love. There was something I had access to and was aware would help them get what they wanted. Looking back now I see how I used content to overdeliver on value by developing this workshop and delivering it thirteen times, in smaller groups to 350 employees. The outcomes of this workshop also made a dent in their goals for improving employee engagement and diversity and inclusion. This demonstrated overdelivering on contribution by focusing on the results and impact that mattered most to these leaders. Finally, by introducing this powerful and empowering Fascinate® test to this team, I connected 350 people to the work and mission of Fascinate Inc.

Eventually, opportunities to speak on stage, facilitate workshops with teams, travel abroad, and a start a full-time business opened for me. This is a testament to what Abraham Lincoln was quoted as saying: "I will study and get ready and perhaps my chance will come."4 A couple of years after this beyond-my-courage-zone moment, I was invited by the Fascinate® team to take all that I was teaching in my workshops and coaching programs and use it to teach others how to do the same. I took on the role of program director for the Fascinate Certified Advisor Program. That was five years ago and I have since trained 150 Fascinate Certified Advisors using the same system I used in my very first workshop.

This was not my original intent. There were no strings attached. My intentions were to overdeliver on value, to bring my Brilliant Difference in the service of others, to help them get what they wanted most. It's by helping others that we get to receive what we most want and need. It is not the other way around. Selling from love invites you to show your work in the spirit of service and the wisdom of love. This is succinctly captured by best-selling author and motivational speaker Brian Tracy: "Love only grows by sharing. You can only have more for yourself by giving it away to others."[5]

Now here are a few more ways that you can apply these ideas:

Content	• Write a blog or article on LinkedIn and tag clients who would benefit. • Share industry reports, white papers, books via email, Slack or snail mail. • Host a seminar with an expert panel addressing an issue your clients are struggling with. Be sure to include other experts who can deliver salient information you don't have. • Deliver a keynote, sit on panel at an industry event. • Host a webinar informing clients of the latest changes in your industry and how to adapt.

Connection	• Set a weekly target to connect two people in your network. • Host a lunch networking party in your home or office. • Host a fundraising dinner on behalf of a top client and invite clients who would benefit from knowing each other. • Participate in events your clients are hosting by bringing people they'd benefit from knowing. • Make referrals to your client's businesses.
Contribution	• Suggest ideas for new products or services your client can offer. • Provide insights on new industries your client can enter to grow market share. • Offer information on how they can improve their company's production rates or efficiencies. • Recommend solutions to improve team engagement and performance. • Make suggestions about how to improve customer service and build loyalty.

Whether you overdeliver by adding value through content, connection, or contribution, it's important to focus on the areas that come easily to you *and* the ones that will serve your client best. Will they benefit more from receiving a relevant book in the mail or from making a connection to a trusted accountant or from an idea on how to manage a new industry regulation? Put yourself in their shoes and choose the one they would benefit most from and that you delight in giving.

Stage 3: Create invitations and enroll clients to work with you: In this stage of the process you've established enough trust and rapport and you're ready to make a commitment to a stronger relationship. You do this by extending an invitation and asking your ideal client to work with you.

When creating an invitation or enrolling an ideal client to work with you, know that much of the heavy lifting has already been done. They've been identified as an ideal client, you've built sufficient trust to have the confidence to ask, and now the time has come. When selling from love, you still may get a bit antsy to make the invitation. It's not out of fear, but excitement. You're what I like to call "nervcited"—a mix of nervousness and excitement that can look like fear. But when coming from love, it's coming from a place where you're jazzed to have an opportunity to use your brilliance to make a difference to others. Don't be disappointed if it doesn't feel easy and effortless all the time; you're still in the zone when you come from love.

Let's look at Anna, a coach who teaches personal branding courses and workshops. She's teaching her most popular personal branding online course. Her course is launching at the end of the month and she wants to have ten people participate in this workshop. She's done lots of work being present on social media and her network. They know she's the "go-to" person for all things personal branding. Over time, she's built a following, an email list, and a list of ideal clients who are interested in and perfect for her workshops.

To create invitations, Anna presents her course to readers of her blog and social media posts. She sends out a few emails to specific people in her circle, informing them about the course and asking if they'd extend the invitation to people in their network who would benefit from it. Anna's email signature line, website, and social media cover pages all have the same message: sign up for this amazing personal branding course. She even sets up an email promotional campaign which is automated through her CRM service provider. Anna has all her bases covered: she's creating awareness and is extending invitations.

But sales aren't coming in as fast and easily as Anna likes. She pulls out her most powerful selling from love tool: moving online relationships offline.

The internet has made selling easier by giving you access to people and places you normally wouldn't have access to. But at the same time, it's made it harder. Getting attention, being noticed, and creating meaningful connection is becoming more difficult as every day goes by. Anna knows this and takes every opportunity to leverage the online connections she's making and moves them offline to build an even deeper relationship.

She does this by extending free personal branding strategy calls. She knows that if she can speak or meet with her ideal clients by phone, video, or in person, she has a better chance of understanding their current challenges and goals and determining if this course would be the solution to help them get what they want. It's also an opportunity for her to strengthen her relationship with them and even give her more practice creating invitations from love.

Anna sets up two days and books ten personal branding strategy calls. Here's what happened out of the ten calls:

- Two ideal clients didn't show up. That was great; they self-selected out of being ideal clients right now and Anna used their appointment time to send out more emails to clients on her interest list.

- Three ideal clients said not now. That was great; they will be first to call next time she offers this course.

- One ideal client said no to the course, but yes to her coaching. That was great; she got a sale on one of her other offers.

- Two ideal clients signed up. That was great; she filled up her course.

- One ideal client said they knew someone who would be perfect for her course. That was great; she got a referral.

- One ideal client said no and that they were 100% clear on their personal brand. That was great; this made her heart warm as this was one more person clear on his value, a mission near and dear to her heart.

What are you noticing?

First: selling from love doesn't mean you'll always get a sale. Selling from love doesn't mean that your ideal clients will love what you're offering, right now or ever. Selling from love is also about not being attached to the outcome. Anna demonstrated that beautifully by being okay, no matter what the outcome of her calls were. It was great either way.

A traditional Taoist story says it best:

"When an old farmer's stallion wins a prize at a country show, his neighbor calls round to congratulate him, but the old farmer says, 'Who knows what is good and what is bad?'

The next day some thieves come and steal his valuable animal. His neighbor comes to commiserate with him, but the old man replies, 'Who knows what is good and what is bad?'

A few days later the spirited stallion escapes from the thieves and joins a herd of wild mares, leading them back to the farm. The neighbor calls to share the farmer's joy, but the farmer says, 'Who knows what is good and what is bad?'

The following day, while trying to break in one of the mares, the farmer's son is thrown and fractures his leg. The neighbor calls to share the farmer's sorrow, but the old man's attitude remains the same as before.

The following week the army passes by, forcibly conscripting soldiers for the war, but they do not take the farmer's son because he cannot walk. The neighbor thinks to himself, 'Who knows what is good and what is bad?' and realizes that the old farmer must be a Taoist sage."[6]

Often, we can fall into the trap that selling is only good when we get the sale. Selling from love is not determined by the outcome or result. Selling from love comes from the intent. Selling from love is good because it comes from love.

CHAPTER ELEVEN: MAKE IT EVEN EASIER FOR YOUR CLIENT TO SPREAD THE LOVE

—

"Every heart sings a song, incomplete, until another heart whispers back. Those who wish to sing always find a song."

Plato

NOW THAT YOU'VE walked an ideal client from being an indifferent outsider to saying yes to working with you, they've become a client. You have gained agreement and established a mutual partnership for working together. When selling from love, even though a sale has happened it doesn't mean your work is over. A client saying yes to your offer can mean they like you, but it may not be enough for them to love you.

When they love you, they're willing to put their reputation on the line for you by becoming a devoted insider. Remember, a devoted insider is someone who's willing to publicly share an association with you. This is a risk: they're putting their name, status, and character out on the limb for you, in front of their inner circle of family, friends, and network. Their voice is coming through the megaphone of love for you.

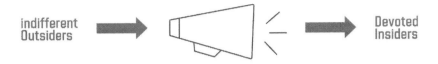

You've probably run into situations where someone has asked you to be a reference, to put a good word in for them or even to pass their resume along to a hiring manager for a job. You had influence over whether or not they could get the job and they wanted your help. If it was someone you respected and knew would do a good job, you'd move forward and pass along the reference or resume. Yet, if it wasn't, you'd cringe at the idea and would think of ways to get out of making the recommendation.

The reference you were making was no longer about them. It was about you and what referring this person would say about you. If they were smart, successful, and respected, by association this would mean that you were someone who is smart, successful, and respected. If they were disorganized, lazy, and unreliable, this association could mean that you are somewhat disorganized, lazy, and unreliable.

Now logically, we can see these two people are completely different but, in the moment, our rational mind is not thinking. Our emotional mind is reacting, and specifically with fear: fear of what people may think of you as a result of your associating with this person by making this referral—this is the driving force behind your decision.

This is what you want to avoid with your clients. You don't want them to forget, think twice, or decline making you their ideal choice to recommend to their network. A devoted insider is someone who has such an affinity for you that they're out there looking for more people to bring into your devoted insider tribe. That is what it means to go from liking to loving you. Best-selling author Seth Godin captures the essence of this brilliantly in his book *This is Marketing*, when he writes: "Loving you is a way of expressing themselves. Becoming part of your moment is an expression of who they are. That love leads to traction, to engagement, and to evangelism. That love becomes part of their identity, a chance to do something that feels right. To express themselves through their contributions, their actions, and the badge they wear. You can't hope that everyone will feel this way, but you can do your work for the people who do."[1]

This love will facilitate the most powerful sell from love strategy that doesn't cost you a dime of your marketing budget—that's word of mouth. Devoted insiders become carriers of your message and instead of one voice doing the telling, you've got multiple voices in living rooms, at kitchen tables, in boardrooms, or at the game, sharing the transformation and impact you've delivered to them. Now let's talk more about how you can create a devoted insider. We'll continue where we left off in Chapter 10 by moving to stage four.

Stage 4: Deliver generously to your client: Now it's time to deliver on your promise. This is where you get to bring your Brilliant Difference, turn on all the bells and whistles, and wow and surprise your client with unexpected positive perks they didn't see coming. You want to guide your client to the outcome and transformation they signed up for and surprise them in extraordinary ways. To be clear, this is not a case of under-promise and overdeliver. You are committed to deliver on your transformation and then something more.

To create devoted insiders, you need to know that the experience you create for your clients is what they will talk about. If you only deliver the goods, that's nothing to write home about. We don't praise an airline because our luggage arrived; that's expected. But if you go above and beyond in ways that they'll never forget, then when your client is at a dinner party with friends and the conversation turns to how their accountant is not hitting the mark or their adviser is not responsive and is nickel and diming them at every corner, they will think of you. They will not only think of you, but they will praise your glories because you do house visits, send birthday cards to every family member of their household, and you even showed up to their family backyard fundraiser.

In a McKinsey study, researchers noted that: "Experiential word of mouth is the most common and powerful form, typically accounting for 50 to 80 percent of word-of-mouth activity in a given product category. It results from a consumer's direct experience with a product or service, largely what that experience deviates from what's expected. (Consumers rarely complain about or praise a company when they receive what they expect.) ... Positive word of mouth, on the other hand, can generate a tailwind for a product or service."[2]

In other words, you need to create experiences your clients will remember and that they'll be willing to talk about while at the same time putting their reputation on the line for you. It's a tall order, but it's doable and achievable.

In Chapter 10 we covered the three ways to overdeliver on value to build trust and engagement: content, connections, and contributions. Each of these overdeliver conduits continues to play a role when delivering generously after the sale has happened. You don't stop courting a client after they sign on the dotted line. As in marriage, date nights are still important even after the wedding. Your investment in your client relationships will pay you dividends over the long haul. Start now so you can benefit from them one day and so your future self doesn't have to work so hard, because your clients will be doing the selling for you.

Back in 2016 I had the opportunity to attend the Disney Institute for a leadership conference to better understand Disney's approach to quality service. One teaching that stuck with me was this: "Go an extra inch, not a mile." Often, we think we need to make big things happen or deliver on some colossal event for our clients to remember. But it's not about how big or grand the value is, but how personal and meaningful it is.

It was the kick-off night of the conference, and all of us attendees were gathered in a large meeting room mingling, with a loud hum of conversation in the room, some enjoying a glass of wine or beer, as the service staff walked around with hors d'hoeuvres.

My phone rang, I stepped outside, and it was my husband on the other end. The first thing he said was "Jelena is fine, but she's in the hospital." My face turned white as snow as I dropped down to sit on the bench behind me.

He further added that she had been at school, had fallen off the monkey bars, and had broken her collar bone. She was resting in the hospital and he assured me she was okay, and they'd be on their way home that evening.

As I re-entered the cocktail area, Garett, a Disney host, opened the door for me. He noticed I was distraught and asked what was wrong. I told him that my little girl was in a hospital 1300 miles away in Ontario with a broken collar bone. He listened and offered a few kind words to ease my stress. Then he went on to tell me about how his daughter had had the exact same injury at about the same age as Jelena and today was attending college on a baseball scholarship. He said, "the broken collar bone made her stronger." He provided comfort, a listening ear, and consolation. Not only that, for the duration of the conference he continued to check in on me, giving me front-line service, making sure I had everything I needed. He even prepared a special gift package with Disney memorabilia to bring home to my little girl.

It wasn't a lot, but it was personal and meaningful. It was something I'll never forget.

Delivering generously is all about the details, being genuine, and creating customized value for your clients now that you know them a whole lot better. When selling from love, delivering generously in personal and meaningful ways brings you one step closer to helping your clients fall in love with you and an opportunity for them to become one of your devoted insiders.

Here are 7 ways you can deliver generously in personal and meaningful ways:

1. Send personalized, handwritten thank you notes and birthday cards. I have a colleague who makes her own cards (she's an artist on the side). A study by analytics and technology provider Fulcrum reported that 75% of customers who received a birthday message from a company with which they did business thought more highly of that company, and that 88% of those with positive responses showed increased brand loyalty.[3]

2. Send small care/gift packages for client milestones—anniversaries, births, new home, new job, or business anniversary.

3. Send a donation to your client's favorite fundraiser.

4. Meet with clients at their place of work or at home.

5. Pop by their office with coffee/tarts for their staff.

6. Add an unexpected bonus to their purchase. Recently I had head shots taken for my website. I purchased a ten-photo package, but when it came time to make my selection the photographer surprised me with ten more and a duplicate series in black and white. That was a pleasant surprise.

7. Provide a follow-up summary of each client meeting capturing key take-aways, next steps, and commitments.

It's the extra inch, not the mile you go that will get you there. Think about this. Water is hot at 211 degrees and at 212 it boils. With boiling water comes steam, steam powerful enough to fuel a locomotive.[4]

Raising the temperature of water by one degree means the difference between something that is very hot and something that generates enough force to power a machine.

The same goes for you: what's the one inch or one degree you could add that will power up your client relationships with enough love that generates devoted insiders for you and your business.

Stage 5: Deepen your client relationship: When selling from love, it's not about being a one-hit wonder. You're in it for the long haul with your client. You're developing a relationship with them and, over time, looking to strengthen and deepen that relationship. When your ideal client meets you for the first time, they've got a specific problem they're looking to have solved. If you're the lucky one they choose, you get to wow them with your Brilliant Difference, facilitate a transformation, and deliver generously in the process. However, as soon as one problem is solved a new one emerges and, as you strengthen your relationship with your client, you need to ask yourself how you could deepen your relationship with them even further by helping them solve the next, new problem that arises.

Let me share how I experienced this "solving one problem always creates another problem to be solved" situation. We moved from the city to the country in the spring of 2015. To get bread that is fresh, crispy on the outside, soft and chewy on the inside, we had to drive twenty-five minutes to the nearest bakery. We were accustomed to walking to a bakery and now it wasn't as accessible or convenient as we were used to. This was our first problem: lack of easy, convenient access to fresh bread.

To solve this first problem, I decided to make bread at home. Well, if you've ever made bread, it takes time and lots of kneading. Now I had a second problem: I didn't have the time to make and wait, nor the interest in kneading my own bread. On top of that, I didn't enjoy the added work of scraping the sticky flour off my kitchen counter.

To solve this second, *new problem* I purchased a bread maker. I'd easily place all my ingredients inside the bread maker's metal basket and, voila, three hours later, fresh from the oven, crispy and soft bread. Now you'd think I had my bread problem solved. But I didn't.

Normally the bread I bought in the bakery was sliced and now I had to slice it myself. Now imagine the crumb party happening all over my counter and floor as a result. My fresh bread problem is solved, and the third *new problem* it created as a result was messy counters and floors.

Consider this: in what ways are you creating new problems for your clients as a direct result of solving their original problem?

When you solve one problem, a new one emerges. It may not happen simultaneously and not for all your clients, but for a select number it will. With my bread problem, there are people who had more time and enjoyed kneading—this would not be a problem for them, so they'd not need a bread maker. For people like me, I needed one. Now, when it came time to slicing, I could have bought a bread slicer to avoid the counter crumb mess. But it would have been more painful listening to my husband give me grief over buying another small kitchen appliance. The pain of crumbs was bearable compared to a nagging husband. Needless to say, I didn't buy the slicer.

Identify your Client's Journey

Taking time to put yourself in your clients' shoes, to see the world through their eyes, is critical in this step. Understanding what they want and need is not something you'll be directing. Your client will be guiding you through. You do have a choice in the matter: you get to choose if you want to solve this next problem with a transformation using your products, services, or expertise.

Your client has already made a big decision and that was deciding to work with you in the first place. Now, how can you validate their choice and solidify their relationship with you by continuing to serve them for their new and emerging needs?

When selling from love you want to make your client sticky. You want them stuck on you. You increase client stickiness by having them choose to work with you over and over again. This means that the products, services, and solutions you offer not only help them solve their current problems, but also the future problems and goals they aren't yet aware of or do not have right now. It's through serving them over and over again that you get to deepen and strengthen this relationship. It's through repeated, continuous contact and transformational delivery that you show them more reasons they should become a devoted insider.

For an accountant, a client may initially come to you to file personal income taxes. Then they decide to open a business and call you to help them set up their corporate papers, annual financial statements, and corporate tax filings. After a few years, because of their business success, they have an interested buyer who wants to acquire their business. As an accountant, you can help them with all the financial aspects of the purchase, but they'll need a business valuation expert and legal advice from a lawyer. This is not a service you provide directly, but you have colleagues you trust in these situations. The client has now sold their business and has come into a significant sum of money and asks you, as their accountant, to set up estate and efficient tax planning strategies to minimize tax implications from the sale of their business.

The client journey map for this accountant's business is as follows:

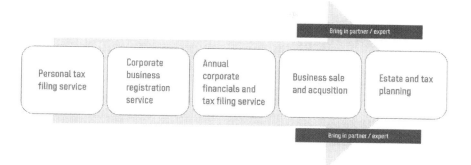

At any given point in this client's journey, the accountant can decide to continue to serve this client or not. The accountant can decide to do only personal income tax filings and provide expert advice on how to minimize taxes, or to follow the client onwards from personal to business taxes and then to estate planning.

As a professional, you get to decide on this. When selling from love, you're always looking to deepen the relationship. You may provide additional services following the client along their journey or you may be the proficient expert that goes deep in one area, such as personal taxes in our accountant's example, and offers various solutions that focus on this specific area.

Here are 5 things you can do to help you identify your client's journey map:

To craft the best journey maps, you should take all the information from your client's mouth. Feedback, focus groups, intake surveys, exit surveys, evaluations, interviews, observations, and social media, all provide venues for you to learn more about what your client needs most.

1. Before you start working with your clients, invite them to complete an intake questionnaire.

2. After you provide a product or service, ask clients to complete an evaluation or assessment of their experience. Be sure to ask them

what they now need after using your product or service or what is top of mind for them now.

3. For clients that leave you or stop buying from you, invite them to complete an exit survey so you can better understand why they're leaving or no longer need you or your services.

4. Become a social media observation ninja. Review forums, groups, or pages where your clients spend time or even check your competitor's page to learn what your ideal and current clients are struggling with and most want solved.

5. When going into a new area or market you've not yet explored, doing one on one interviews or gathering a few people in a focus group is a great start. Discussing the challenges they're experiencing and what they want solved at this time is always a valuable exercise to understand better what is top of mind for them.

Defining your client journey map is informed by your client's needs. However, you get to decide to which area of the journey you want to apply your Brilliant Difference and deliver transformative results.

Stage 6: Assemble sell from love ambassadors and advocates: Devoted insiders spread your message and are carriers of your work and impact into their homes, office buildings, and network. They are your word-of-mouth marketing. Why is word of mouth so effective? Well, for starters, when a friend, relative, or colleague makes a recommendation, it carries weight. You trust them more than the ad that crosses your Facebook or Instagram feed. Secondly, word of mouth is personal and specific. There are two reasons devoted insiders will share or make a recommendation to someone they know: because it makes them look good and because a person they care about is struggling with a problem they know someone in their circle can help them solve.

The first reason is more about the person making the recommendation for sure, but it's still a valid reason. It's by associating themselves with you that they get to tell the world who they are. You've seen those overt name droppers, brand-name label wearers, or even those who can't wait to tell you they heard about an exclusive sale, event, or opportunity. This is word of mouth by association. It tells the world who they are, because of the people they hang out with, buy from, support, and are willing to put their reputation on the line for. The second reason is not so much about the person making the referral, but about the person receiving it.

Perhaps a friend is complaining about the various investment statements that flood their mailbox and don't know what they have or if they're making the most of their money. In this instance, if you have an awesome, amazing, out-of-this-world financial adviser, you bet you're going to tell your friend about them. Or let's say you've got a colleague who threw his back out at a golf game and is having a hard time moving around the office—you wouldn't hesitate to recommend the osteopath who changed your life five years ago. And finally, let's say you've got a client who's looking to enhance processes through digital transformation and you've got a colleague who does this specific work—you jump right in, singing their praises with a recommendation.

We only tell people about a product, service, or solution when someone is specifically complaining about a problem he or she is having. Word of mouth is targeted, personal, and specific. Your message is being shared to the right audience: your ideal client.

To generate ambassadors and advocates, you need to identify ideal clients in the pool of indifferent outsiders. Then these ideal clients trust you enough to say yes to becoming a client and working with you. Over time, as you continue to strengthen this bond by being generous with your time, resources, knowledge, and love, they get to fall in love with you. And one day, if you're lucky enough, you get the honor of having a devoted insider.

Remember this: you don't need *all* indifferent outsiders to become your client and all clients will not love you enough to become a devoted insider. And that's okay. You don't need them all. You start with one.

Can You Measure Love?

I've spent most of my career in financial services. We had what was called Net Promoter Score (NPS) as a metric to measure client loyalty. An outside agency would call clients and interview them to get feedback on their experience. There'd be a series of questions they'd ask to better understand the value they received, if they encountered a problem, how and if it was resolved, and if they felt heard and understood. But the ultimate question that measured the NPS metric was this: would you recommend the bank to family and friends?

NPS measures love. NPS measures the likelihood and willingness of your clients to spread the love on your behalf through word of mouth. It's a valid metric to help you learn if your clients are willing to put their name on the line for you to their inner circle. Will your name and your company be the first recommendation they make to their friends? NPS helps you identify devoted insiders.

NPS is calculated by asking clients if they'd recommend you or your company to family and friends after they've had an experience with you. A client would respond to this question based on a score ranging from 0-10.

Getting a 9 or 10 = A Promoter. This is someone who would definitely recommend you. They are a devoted insider, advocate, and willing messenger to spread the love of your work.

Getting a 7 or 8 = A Passive. This is someone who may or may not recommend you. They are not a devoted insider. They'll hesitate, give a second thought, or may not even remember that you're the person who could help one of their inner-circle people. It's nothing against you or your products, services, or expertise. They are neutral. They are not standing up on a soap box for you, nor are they calling the better business bureau to complain either. They are your "meh" type of client. You have not yet done enough to wow them or have them love you or they might just not love you, which is also okay too.

Getting a 0 to 6 = A Detractor. This is someone who will not recommend you. They may not have anything against you. They could just be the type of person who doesn't recommend anything to anyone, because it's not something they do. Or they may have had an experience with you or your company that didn't go well. They left unsatisfied or unhappy with their results or experience. Some will even get on a soap box and declare their dislike and unhappiness with you and your company. We don't want detractors. The fewer the better. They slow and impede growth, can damage your brand, and stop the spread of love through word of mouth.

Your NPS will translate to more sales and revenue growth. More promoters mean you'll save on marketing costs and improve productivity and efficiency costs. In a study done by Satmetrix, they showed the value of improving client experience and its effect on the bottom line[5]:

- 20% to 60% in organic growth is accounted for by Net Promoter Score

- 30% better conversion rate for referral leads

- 2% increase in customer retention which has the same effect as decreasing costs by 10%

Focusing on your client experiences and measuring loyalty with this simple question, "would you recommend us to family and friends?", will help you know exactly how much love your clients have for you.

The NPS score is calculated by taking the percentage of promoters you have and subtracting them from the percentage of your detractors. Passives are not included, as they are neutral. For instance, if you surveyed 100 clients and received 52 promoters, 40 passive, and 8 detractors, your NPS score would be: 44 (52% promoters – 8% detractors). Is 44% a good number or a bad one?

You can check out industry standards to see where you land relative to your competitors. Certain industries such as specialty stores, tablet computers, and online shopping will have a higher NPS score than your internet service or cable TV provider. The more specialized your offering is, the more likely you will generate more promoters than a mass market, commoditized solution. With a commodity-type solution, there are way too many fish in the sea already serving everyone. You want to be a big fish in a small pond. You want to bring something special to a specific someone. When you do this, you give them something to write home about.

This is where selling from love can make all the difference. When you sell from love you have a Brilliant Difference that is unique, special, and personal. You have a genuine interest, care, and compassion for the client, the human being behind the number. You have a product, service, and expertise that is ready to deliver a transformation. You have a solution that you inherently believe will help your people get what they most want. You subscribe to the notion that your client gets to become more of who they are, because you've had the honor of taking part in their journey. Selling from love is not a sales strategy, process, or model. Selling from love is a way of being.

CHAPTER TWELVE:
BE OPEN AND WILLING
TO RECEIVE LOVE

—

"Because one believes in oneself, one doesn't try to convince others.
Because once one is content with oneself, one doesn't need others' approval.
Because one accepts oneself, the whole world accepts him or her."

Lao Tzu

ELLING YOUR PRODUCT generates an opportunity for you to benefit. You earn money, bonuses, rewards, accolades, recognition, and even gain status as a result of selling. You already know that when selling from love, you need to put your clients' interests ahead of your own, focus on what's in it for them, and have the ability to see the world through their eyes. Now, how do you put your clients first while acknowledging you have an interest and a desire to benefit from the sale? How do you honor their interests while still honoring yours?

Allowing Yourself to Receive

One of the biggest blocks holding us back from reaching our full potential of happiness, success, and fulfillment is giving our self permission to receive the benefits of our selling efforts. Selling from love invites you to allow yourself to receive the rewards that come from selling. Selling from love invites you to receive *unconditionally*. It ultimately asks you to love yourself so much that you allow yourself to benefit fully from your selling efforts.

That's what I love about this approach. Selling from love is about serving more clients with your products and services and it's a journey of personal growth and self-acceptance. It's a call to remember that you are a complete, capable, and worthy person. You are here to express and experience who you truly are and receive all the goodness, rewards, and benefits that come along with it. Selling from love offers you a way to do just that.

Selling from love does not mean you are using the act of selling to find yourself or to love yourself through a sale or the result of it. It's easy to fall into this trap. When we close a sale or achieve our sales and revenue goals, we feel good and attribute our value to getting results. When a sale doesn't close or we're challenged to hit targets, we internalize it to mean something is wrong with us or that we're not enough.

Selling from love isn't about your performance because you're already valuable and worthy—selling from love gives you an opportunity to experience this truth, again and again. That's the difference. When selling from love you don't want to put your interests ahead of your clients', and you don't want to validate your worth with your results, but you do want to receive openly the rewards that come your way. You are open—but not attached—to the outcome of your selling efforts.

Expanding Your Love Range: How Much Are You Willing to Love Yourself?

In his book *The Big Leap*, Gay Hendricks talks about the "upper limit problem"[1]. An upper limit problem is like an invisible glass ceiling you hit when you exceed how much happiness, success, and fulfillment you allow yourself to have.

Each of us has a limit on how much good we allow ourselves to enjoy. It sounds ridiculous, doesn't it? Still, it's true. Fear of failure, rejection, and judgment can be why you hold yourself back from more of what you want. But fear of success is the greatest fear that hides and haunts many of us. Why wouldn't you want to have all the happiness life has to offer? For starters, somewhere along the way you learned to believe you didn't deserve it. Remember, our brains like to play it safe, to choose certainty over uncertainty, comfort over courage, fear over love, because it's what we know and what we're used to, even if we find it stifling.

When you get to your upper limit, you move out of your comfort zone and inadvertently do something to stop the positive forward trajectory and stay put. That something sabotages your fulfillment because it's out of your normal experience. You may get into a fight with your partner the night before the biggest sales presentation of your career. You're emotionally drained and don't get enough sleep, which prevents you from nailing your pitch. Or you decide to move forward on an inspiring business idea that would place you as an industry leader and make you lots of money. Suddenly your calendar fills up with current client demands and volunteer commitments, leaving you no time to bring your big idea to fruition.

Remember in Chapter 3 where we talked about moving from your comfort zone to your courage zone? Here's an additional way to make that move: increase your upper limit. When an opportunity comes along to experience a higher degree of success, you're being invited to move into your courage zone. You've got a chance in this courage zone moment to love yourself more than you ever have and to raise the upper limit of what you allow yourself to receive.

Selling from love gives you an opportunity to make that move. Selling from love helps you revisit your beliefs regarding how much happiness, success, and fulfillment you deserve. Selling from love helps you learn how to increase your upper limit—while serving your clients!

A Courage Zone Moment: Learning to Receive Happiness, Success, and Fulfillment

I was in grade three and our teacher had divided us into three different reading groups based on our individual skill level. I was in the middle group. Each day we gathered in our small reading groups to read aloud excerpts from a story book. Over time my reading improved, and the teacher moved me up to the level one group. As I approached the small group of level one readers, Tina, the top student in the class, looked over at me and asked with a better-than-thou tone, "What are *you* doing here?" I proudly replied (with a big smile): "Ms. Yates moved me up to this group now." Tina then said five words that would reverberate throughout the rest of my life: "Oh, you *finally* made it."

Finally made it? What did she mean by that? Right before that moment, I had believed I deserved to be in that level one reading group. I had worked hard, improved, and earned a spot in that circle. But right after those words, I felt deflated of any goodness, pride, and joy I was feeling. All the work, effort, and improvement I had made didn't matter because I should have been there sooner.

I didn't realize it at the time, but this grade three event created an upper limit problem. "Finally making it" meant that I didn't deserve to be there, because I had to learn, practice, and work to get there. It often informed and influenced how I showed up in future courage zone moments. If I had a chance to work with a big client, speak on stage, or present a proposal to a high stake's influencer, Tina's remark, buried somewhere in my subconscious mind, would poke its head up, making me feel as though I didn't belong and was not worthy, as I did in my grade three reading circle.

Over time, those protection strategies we talked about in Chapter 3—perfection, performing, and proving—took hold of me. My thought was that if I delivered perfect work, performed to meet and exceed expectations, and proved that I was worthy to be in the room, then I would avoid judgment and show them all I did belong.

Some of the stories I've shared with you already—such as the resume download at the conference where I needed to prove my value to Sandra, or the Year of Yes which led to overcommitment and burnout—were examples of an upper limit problem. Underneath it all, I had this belief that if I had to work at the skill, credentials, or experience, then I didn't deserve to be in the room. I held myself back and limited how much success I allowed myself to have.

My real courage zone moment wasn't getting on stage to speak to hundreds of people. It was learning to love myself enough to believe I deserved to be there.

Selling from love will help you heal those past unacknowledged wounds which are holding you back from living out your full potential. Once you heal those wounds, you can receive all the happiness, success, and fulfillment you desire. It comes when you accept and love yourself, just the way you are.

Who's in the Driver's Seat?

When we're kids, most of us don't learn how to deal with the difficult stuff that happens to us. For many of us, doing whatever we can to bottle up or push away an unwanted feeling or negative experience is the only option we know. As a result, we don't end up learning how to process, or even feel, uncomfortable emotions.

This is important to understand because the reaction you're having to a selling situation is *not* always based on what is happening in the moment, but rather on a past event. These past events accumulate, and they influence how much love and success you allow yourself to experience. Painful or scary events happen, you develop beliefs about these events, and these beliefs then limit how much happiness and love you believe you deserve and thus allow yourself to have. What you've been used to having is in your comfort zone of love and anything beyond that is in your courage zone. When an opportunity shows up for us to love ourselves even more, we activate an upper limit problem and subconsciously orchestrate an event to bring us back within our comfort zone range of love.

Let's say you're getting ready to ask a client to work with you and you get cold feet. You tell yourself the timing isn't right; this client will be too much of a headache or the business will be too big for you to manage. You're looking for reasons why right now is not a good time to ask for the business. You know what it's like to feel the sting of no. Rejection is terribly painful and why the heck would you expose yourself to that again.

These past events are stored in your brain under the file of "rejection" and include when you asked a client for a referral and they didn't respond, when you asked a client to work with you and they said not now or you're too expensive, when you asked a client to try out a new service and they said no.

And it's not only the events of last week, last month, or last year—your file of rejection has entries far older, like the time at your grade eight dance when you mustered up the courage to ask Claudia, the popular girl, to dance. Palms sweaty, heart palpating, you walked up to her and asked. She looked at you with disgust, blurted out a loud "No way," and walked away, giggling with her friends. You raced out of the gym humiliated. Thank goodness, it was the end of the year, summer vacation began, and you could hope that Claudia and her friends would forget by the time high school started in the fall.

But it's not forgotten by your unconscious. Experiences like these can get stuck in you.

Instead of your wise, adult self being in the driver's seat, making decisions and taking action, your younger self moves in and takes over. At thirteen, you didn't have the capability to process those harsh feelings. It's always hard to feel the terrible stuff. Even as adults, we're not very good at it.

This event could also create a belief that girls like Claudia don't say yes to someone like you. You may tell yourself this client you're preparing to make an offer to may be out of your league, too good, too smart, too successful to work with someone like you. You've developed a threshold of how much happiness, success, and fulfillment you allow yourself to have and you believe you deserve.

You've moved on from this grade eight dance moment, but your emotional self has not. Now, as a professional you're putting yourself out there and when it comes to making the ask, you hesitate, because you know what it's like to get a no. Your thirteen-year-old self asking Claudia to dance lingers in the background as you attempt to ask a client to do business with you. In order to protect yourself from having this experience again, your younger self jumps in the driver's seat.

Over your lifetime, based on the life experiences you've had, you've taught yourself that you are worthy enough to experience only a certain amount of fulfillment. Selling from fear will make sure you stay within that limit.

Allow Yourself to Receive Your Money's Worth

When selling, one of the biggest obstacles my coaching clients tell me they face is what to charge. They ask me questions such as:

- How do you set your prices, especially fees for your services like advice, coaching, and consulting?

- How do you stop billing for hours and start being rewarded for true value?

- How do you make more money doing work you love?

Money carries a ton of baggage. We all have stories about money that come from what your upbringing was, how much or how little money you had, and your current relationship with money. Money is how you get paid for your services, it is the result of your selling activities, and money is what puts food on the table, cars in the driveway, and tells the world who we are based on all the things we have.

Depending on your background and relationship with money, often an old story will show up and your younger self moves into your driver's seat. You'll especially notice this in moments when you're moving out of your comfort zone. If you grew up in a home where you parents lived paycheque to paycheque, you may also notice a similar theme happening in your life. Your ten-year-old self has the wheel in your thirty-year-old self's situation.

For instance, you're knocking out your sales targets; bonuses and awards are coming your way. You've got more money coming in than ever before. The problem is, it's going out just as fast. Even with oodles of money, you're still living paycheque to paycheque. No matter what bonus you receive or how much money you make, you tend to not have enough. You go back to the same theme.

Somewhere along the line, you decided you only deserved to have a certain amount of money. This was taught to you growing up and it's been a story you've continued to tell yourself. It's showing up in your business and selling.

Selling from love is a beautiful practice. It's a method that uses selling to look at those old stories that insist you only deserve a limited amount of happiness, success, fulfillment, love, and money. Selling from love is a way for you to reclaim your true worth and be rewarded for the value you bring to the clients you serve. Selling from love invites you to love yourself so much that you allow yourself to let go of the old stories of comfort. You embrace your new story of courage, worth, and love.

Take for instance my client Brooke. She's been a financial adviser for more than two decades and is one of the few advisers who charges a financial planning fee to her clients. This is Brooke's Brilliant Difference, it's her most valuable asset and what her client's profit from most. They can get stock picks, mutual fund recommendations, and investment analytics from any other financial adviser. But the way Brooke guides, advises, and provides her service, her financial planning, the way she builds her client relationships and delivers results is unique. No one does it the way Brooke does, and no one ever will. This is her unique advantage and her Brilliant Difference. This is what she does best and what her clients value most from her, so much so that they are willing to pay a fee to get it.

Brooke is clear and confident in her value. She knows she's worth her fee in spades. This does not come from a place of ego; it comes from a place of deep knowing and service. This knowing didn't come easily for Brooke. For a chunk of her career she didn't charge fees, nor did she have good boundaries with her clients. They'd call her at all hours of the day, and she'd do whatever it took to make them happy.

She's done some heavy lifting through self-awareness, self-reflection, and self-management. Brooke had a narrative that she wasn't worth investing in. Her eighteen-year-old self was in the driver's seat of her forty-five-year-old self's career. The year she graduated high school, her parents decided to use the money they saved for her college education to buy an extravagant vacation home. The story that was buried deep within Brooke was that she wasn't worth educating, that a vacation home was more important and more valuable than she was. This story was showing up at her work as a financial adviser and it was affecting the sales she was getting, the money she was making, and the lifestyle she was living.

Brooke didn't believe she was worthy and as a result would waive fees, bend over backwards for her clients, and devalue her counsel. Then Brooke did the work. She dug up this old story and started telling herself a new one.

Brooke figured out her value and has her adult self in the driver's seat. Today she isn't attaching her worth to whether or not clients buy from her. She is clear and confident on the transformation and outcomes she promises to deliver to her clients. When you're that sure, it's in your bones and you've moved to a natural state of knowing and valuing your worth.

During a recession, when getting new clients is most challenging, Brooke didn't do what most of her colleagues did: discount or completely waive their fees. She was bidding on a new $1.5 million account. The client wanted to work with her, but his sticking point was the financial planning fee. He asked that she waive it and challenged her by saying her competitors were not charging a fee. Brooke knew her value and that she was worthy of the fee she charged. She did not need her client or the sale to validate her or her Brilliant Difference.

She clearly explained to her prospect the value she brought and the benefit he would receive as a result. She walked in with a sense that if he hired her or not, the outcome didn't define her worth. She was already worthy. She wanted her client to find the right financial adviser and that would mean she could not compromise on who she was and the value she brought.

Ultimately, the client did decide to work with Brooke and transferred his entire portfolio to her. The lesson here is not that she got the sale, which was great news, but that the sale didn't define her identity or determine her value or worth. She already knew who she was and that she deserved it.

How to Allow Yourself to Have More Love

What do you do when you find yourself butting up against a limiting story of how much happiness, success, and fulfillment you deserve? How do you expand how much love you will allow yourself to have?

First you notice your story. We cannot repair something if we don't acknowledge that it isn't working. If you aren't getting the sales you want, the recognition or promotions, if revenues aren't coming in and helping you grow, it can be a sign to investigate if you're having an upper limit problem.

You deserve all the happiness, success, fulfillment, love, and money you desire. At the same time what you want is out of your comfort zone. Even if what you want is better than what you currently have, our brains prefer familiarity and comfort, even if this comfort blocks your growth and gives you a life or a business that is far less than what you want. Selling from love invites you to:

- let go of old stories that are no longer serving you

- start telling yourself new stories that strengthen your belief and worthiness

- increase your capacity to hold more happiness, success, and fulfillment

- be open to allow yourself to receive the goodness life has to offer

- ultimately, remind yourself that you are already worthy and deserve to be loved

Selling from love is a practice that increases the limit of happiness you allow yourself to express and experience. To elevate this threshold of love, here are a few methods to navigate:

#1 Feel the FUDGE: Fear, Uncertainty, Doubt, Guilt, Expectations

Part of the problem is we avoid feeling the hard stuff. We deny it's even there. There's a powerful book called *Feel the Fear and Do it Anyway* by Susan

Jeffers[2]. I love the message of this title: Feel the fear, uncertainty, doubt, guilt, and expectations, but don't let them hold you back. Keep on moving and do it anyway. If you call out the uncomfortable and often negative feeling by naming it, feeling it in your body, or spending a few minutes writing about it, you've allowed yourself to feel it. By doing this you limit the power it has over you. You are better in control of the decisions you make and you get to be in the driver's seat.

#2 Feel the Outcome

This is all about replacing the feeling you don't want with the feeling you do want. You can only do this after you've gone through feeling FUDGE. Selling from love is not about masking a hard and difficult feeling with a good feeling, it's about lovingly feeling the hard stuff and using that to move toward feeling the good stuff. Here you're connecting to the fulfillment and love you want to feel when you achieve the outcome you are moving toward right now in this moment.

This is a game changer. Thoughts that are fused with feelings have the power to up your limit to receive and help you sell from love while growing in happiness and satisfaction. Visualizing your ideal outcome, being willing to move toward it, while affirming it with supporting words and thoughts, will be exponentially accelerated when you associate with what it would feel like to have it.

#3 Be Open to Receive

Changing a limiting belief can be challenging. They are so ingrained in your subconscious that you may not even be aware that a limiting belief is holding you back. All you know is that something isn't working in your business or life. That's where you need to be willing to see, willing to change, and willing to do things another way, so you can create the outcome you want.

This is an opportune time to use the positive-power primer practice we talked about in Chapter 4 to expand your willingness and openness to receive. Recite these daily as you navigate your way to expanding how much love you allow yourself to have:

I am willing to allow myself to be open to receive all the happiness, success, and fulfillment available for me to express and experience.

I choose to allow myself to be open to receive all the happiness, success, and fulfillment available for me to express and experience.

I believe I can allow myself to be open to receive all the happiness, success, and fulfillment available for me to express and experience.

I am allowing myself to be open to receive all the happiness, success, and fulfillment available for me to express and experience.

#4 Tell Yourself a New Story

Pay attention to the thoughts in your head about your circumstances. Are you saying things like selling is hard, this will never work, they'll say no? Start telling yourself a new story.

I'm willing to give this a try. It may not work, but I'll give it my best shot. I'm sure I'll get something out of it. If I learn something new, it was worth doing it. Selling is fun, I get to talk to people, help them, and solve problems.

The current stories running through your head became beliefs because you told them to yourself repeatedly. Being mindful of your thoughts and feelings and having a meditation practice are good ways to catch yourself in these old limiting beliefs. To reprogram old default narratives into new empowering ones, you need to do the same thing but in a different direction: tell yourself positive, empowering, and generative stories over and over again.

#5 Stand in a Posture of Non-attachment

The reason we run into a problem is that we attach our worth and value to an outcome of a sale, a client's feedback, or a "like" or comment in a social media post. We look for our identity and validate our worth in the things outside of ourselves instead of understanding who we already are and acknowledging that we're already worthy, valued, and valuable.

When presenting, proposing, or putting yourself out there, do so with non-attachment to a specific outcome. Set an intention to add value, be of service, share a new perspective, or offer your product—but don't be attached to making a meaning or defining a specific outcome. Whether or not they like it, buy it, or recommend it, doesn't define your worth.

Selling from love may or may not get you the sale. But selling from love will give you an opportunity to love yourself even more than you ever have and allow you to have the happiness you want and deserve. Selling from love invites you to ask, "How much are you willing to love yourself, love your client, and love your offer?"

EPILOGUE

___

Moving Forward From Love

You made it! Now that you're at the end, I'm sure you've come to realize that this book is not only about selling, even though it will help you sell better and sell more. Sell From Love is here to help you use the power of selling to be who you really are, so you can become who you're here to be. You get to use selling as a way to get there. I'm reminded by a saying: "How you do anything is how you do everything."[1] This is what I see selling from love offering you. When you learn to sell from love you will not only transform your selling, your business, your results, and your impact, you will also ultimately learn how to:

- Love yourself.

- Honor your talents, skills, and special gifts.

- Move from comfort to courage.

- Be present, pause to listen, and sit in wonder and curiosity.

- Move from self-interest to others' interests.

- See the world through someone else's eyes.

- Turn a transaction into a transformation.

- Craft a message that others will understand.

- Create purpose and meaning in your work.

- Be seen and make yourself visible.

- Gather a group of thoughtful, like-spirited leaders.

- Claim your value and remember you're already worthy.

Selling from love is not something you do. It's who you are.

Where Do You Go From Here?

My belief is that learning doesn't happen in an instant by reading a book or taking a course. Learning happens over time as you take this approach and these ideas and methods into your selling experiences. This is the best way to learn, by using it, practicing it, and making it your own. If you haven't already, access the following resources to continue your journey and deepen your learning on how to sell from love:

1. **Sell From Love Test**: A diagnostic tool to help you assess where you are and where you're not selling from love. You'll quickly uncover what areas are key for you to focus on, so you can sell with more authenticity, create transformations for your clients, and find more meaning, impact, and success when selling your ideas and services. Take the Sell From Love Test at www.sellfromlove.com/test.

2. **Sell From Love Workbook:** This book is filled with practical, immediately implementable ideas and solutions. The workbook is designed to help you take the insights and ideas shared here and apply them directly to your leadership and business. Download the Sell From Love Workbook at www.sellfromlove/workbook.

3. **Sell From Love Community:** Putting yourself out there, selling and marketing your products, services, and expertise, running a business,

and standing up in your leadership takes courage, conviction, and commitment. You don't need to go it alone. This community is here to support you as you implement your ideas, stay consistent, and remain dedicated to your commitment to sell from love. Join the Sell From Love Community at www.sellfromlove.com/community.

At the beginning of this book my promise was to offer you a new way to sell, a way that doesn't use fear tactics or self interest, or dismisses the human behind the numbers. The world needs a more conscious, compassionate, and caring sales model. The world needs you to bring your authentic, true self alongside your special gifts. We need your Brilliant Difference. We need you to bring it, because there are people, your clients, waiting for you to help them make a positive change in their businesses and lives. They need you to take them from a transaction to a transformation in their businesses and lives. This is how you get to make a meaningful difference, live out your big why, and bring more purpose and impact to the world. Selling from love is about falling in love with yourself, your client, and your offer so that you can become the beacon of light the world needs right now.

The End.

RECOMMENDED READING

—

BOOKS HAVE BEEN my mentors along the way to learn how to sell from love. The knowledge and wisdom I've gained through the words of these impeccable authors has been immeasurable. I value learning and reading as a fundamental way to gain ideas, insights, and inspiration. Last year alone I donated 400 books from my personal library. Here are the ones that specifically influenced my journey and learning to sell from love.

- *The War of Art: Break Through the Blocks and Win Your Inner Creative Battles* by Steven Pressfield

- *The Big Leap* by Gay Hendricks

- *How the World Sees You* by Sally Hogshead

- *This Is Marketing: You Can't Be Seen Until You Learn to See* by Seth Godin

- *Tribes: We Need You to Lead Us* by Seth Godin

- *The Dip* by Seth Godin

- *Permission Marketing: Turning Strangers Into Friends And Friends Into Customers* by Seth Godin

- *Building a Storybrand* by Donald Miller

- *Transformational Speaking: If You Want to Change the World, Tell a Better Story* by Gail Larsen

- *The Surrender Experiment: My Journey into Life's Perfection* by Michael Singer

- *A New Earth* by Eckhart Tolle

- *Taking the Leap: Freeing Ourselves from Old Habits and Fears* by Pema Chodron

- *When Things Fall Apart: Heart Advice for Difficult Times* by Pema Chodron

- *The Places That Scare You: A Guide to Fearlessness in Difficult Times* by Pema Chodron

- *Give and Take* by Adam Grant

- *The Go Giver* by Bob Burg and John David Mann

- *Quiet Leadership* by David Rock

- *Ego is the Enemy* by Ryan Holiday

- *Perennial Seller* by Ryan Holiday

ACKNOWLEDGMENTS

—

BEFORE WRITING THIS book, I'd often wonder why an author's acknowledgment list was so long. They were the writer, so how could so many other people be part of the process? Now, standing at the end of this project, I can see how this book could not have been written on my own. It truly took a village. *Sell From* Love was a labor of love that was embraced by so many that came before this book and by all who were part of the journey throughout the writing of it.

First, I'd like to thank Jennifer Louden. The ideas that were once in my mind and heart would not have made it to these pages without your guidance, wisdom, and tender tough love. Thank you for championing this mission when I lost my way and for challenging me to be better because of it. I became a better writer and will forever be grateful to you for helping me create this body of work. A special thank you to Jennifer's Writer's Mastermind for cheering me on throughout this whole process in the forum and through our weekly peer reading pages. Your voice and validation kept me plugging along and moving forward. A special mention thank you goes out to Lynn Jennings and Jenny Grill for your ongoing support. If you have a book in you or don't know where to start, you need to check out Jennifer at www. jenniferlouden.com. She'll help you make it happen.

To my editors Katie Zdybel, Lise Gunby and Monique van den Heuvel: because of your invaluable suggestions and counsel this book is friendlier and richer to read. Thank you for reminding me that it's the detail that makes a good idea an exceptional one.

To my publishing partner Chrissy Hobbs and the Indie Publishing Group. Thank you for your guidance and hand holding every step of the way. You filled this personal courage zone moment with comfort and ease with your experience and expertise. Thank you for your patience and understanding.

To my beta readers Doug Palmer, Janet Lee, Sandra Corelli, and Karen Sawyer: you took the time out of your already full schedules and lives to read this book. Your thoughtful feedback and invitation to share more personal stories made this message clearer and more compelling. Thank you for challenging and supporting me throughout this process.

To my clients, colleagues, and peers who made this book better because of your support, experience, and stories, I am so grateful: Sandra Nesbit, Tara McMullin, David Keesee, Michelle Arpin Begina, Amber Hurdle, Susan Stageman, Kate Bonnycastle, Michelle Peros, Cara Forte, and Heather Korol.

To the Fascinate® team and Fascinate Certified Advisors: thank you for inviting me into your business and lives. You continue to inspire me to find ways to sell from love.

To my Sell from Love Mastermind, Andrea Wenburg, Catalina Valencia, Christi Ratcliff, Heather Taylor, Janet Lee, JeNae Johnson, Kelly Smales, Lisa Hutcheson, Michelle Lopez, and Vicki Hanson-Burkhart: your openness, willingness, and commitment to your work is ever inspiring. Thank you for creating an environment that demonstrated the power, potential, and possibility of what happens when we sell from love. I am sincerely grateful to you for sharing your wisdom, heart, and love.

This book was written in the cracks of my already full and fulfilling life. These cracks were made possible because my husband would take on our farm and life's to-do's,- so that I could write and create this book. Thank you for holding down the fort and making sure life as we know it ran smoothly. I realize I put a lot on us and am deeply grateful for all the work and effort you put into our family and life. For those moments when I lost my way and doubted myself, I can't thank you enough for pulling me up and out. Knowing you were by my side made it easier and was often the fuel I needed to keep going. I truly feel blessed and am grateful to walk alongside you in this crazy life we've created.

To my one and only daughter, Jelena. Who I am today is made possible because of you. You continue to inspire me to be a better human and to continue to learn and grow. You've shown me how to love and be courageous. Each time you've fallen off your horse and gotten back on, I remember to get back on mine. You've been a friend and confidante throughout this entire process. You offer me a safe place to be me, with no judgement, only love. Thank you for picking me as your mom. I won the lottery!

Finally, to you, dear reader, thank you for picking up this book and following along the sell from love roadmap. Your voice and work matter. There are people waiting for you to bring your Brilliant Difference. Trust yourself and know when you come from a place of authenticity, empathy, and purpose, you are aligned to who you are and to love itself. Put one foot in front of the other, keep moving, and let's build a better life and world together from love.

NOTES

—

1. Bible

Introduction

1. "Why Companies are Becoming B Corporations," https://hbr.org/2016/06/why-companies-are-becoming-b-corporations.

2. "How well do your salespeople understand your buyers?" The Business Journals, Doug Winter, https://www.bizjournals.com/bizjournals/how-to/marketing/2015/02/how-well-do-your-salespeople-understand-buyers.html

3. "Putting Purpose to Work: A study of purpose in the workplace," https://www.pwc.com/us/en/purpose-workplace-study.html

4. Putting Purpose to Work: A study of purpose in the workplace, https://www.pwc.com/us/en/purpose-workplace-study.html

5. "U.S. Companies Losing Customers As Consumers Demand More Human Interaction, Accenture Strategy Study Finds,"https://newsroom.accenture.com/news/us-companies-losing-customers-as-consumers-demand-more-human-interaction-accenture-strategy-study-finds.htm

Chapter One: Fall in Love With You

1. Behind the Name, https://www.behindthename.com/name/finka

2. *Average to A+*, Alex Linley, CAPP Press

Chapter Two: Find Your Words to Love

1. Mehrabian's communication study, http://changingminds.org/explanations/behaviors/body_language/mehrabian.htm

2. "Closing the Sale: 6 Tips From Sales Pros," https://www.salesforce.com/blog/2016/10/3-critical-tips-for-closing-the-sale.html

3. *Think and Grow Rich*, Napoleon Hill, Penguin Group

Chapter Three: Move from Comfort to Courage with Love

1. "Stop Overdoing Your Strengths," https://hbr.org/2009/02/stop-overdoing-your-strengths

Chapter Four: Use Self-love to Create Comfort in your Courage Zone

1. "Conceptual Priming," https://www.behavioraleconomics.com/resources/mini-encyclopedia-of-be/priming-conceptual/

2. "Confidence," https://www.dictionary.com/browse/confidence?s=t

CHAPTER FIVE: MASTER THE SELL FROM LOVE SKILLS

1. *To Sell is Human* by Daniel Pink, Riverhead Books, Penguin Group

2. Oprah Winfrey, https://www.youtube.com/watch?v=rw9c8CSnDaU

3. "4 Steps to Having More 'Aha' Moments," https://hbr.org/2016/10/4-steps-to-having-more-aha-moments

Chapter Seven: Love the Transformation, Not Only the Transaction

1. "What Customers Want from Your Products," https://hbswk.hbs.edu/item/what-customers-want-from-your-products

Chapter Nine: Fall in Love With Your Offer

1. *Go Put Your Strengths to Work*, Marcus Buckingham, Free Press

Chapter Ten: Make it Easy for Clients to Find a Way to Love You

1. *The Marquis of Lossie*, George Macdonald, Prince Classics

2. *Influence*, Robert Cialdini, Harper Business

3. *Give and Take*, Adam Grant, Penguin Books

4. "Abraham Lincoln," https://lincolnarchives.com/LincolnQuotes.php

5. Brian Tracy, https://www.goodreads.com/quotes/459366-love-only-grows-by-sharing-you-can-only-have-more

6. "Who Knows What is Good and What is Bad," https://www.movebeyond.net/live-your-dream/who-knows-what-is-good-and-what-is-bad/

Chapter Eleven: Make it Even Easier for Your Client to Spread the Love

1. *This is Marketing*, Seth Godin, Penguin Random House LLC

2. "A new way to measure word-of-mouth marketing," McKinsey & Company, https://www.mckinsey.com/business-functions/marketing-and-sales/our-insights/a-new-way-to-measure-word-of-mouth-marketing

3. "6 Ways to Build Customer Loyalty at Every Touch Point," https://www.convinceandconvert.com/online-customer-experience/build-customer-loyalty/

4. 212 The Extra Degree, Sam Parker, The Walk the Talk Company

5. N.I.C.E. Satmetrix, U.S Consumer 2019 Net Promoter Benchmarks

Chapter Twelve: Be Open and Willing to Receive Love.

1. *The Big Leap*, Gay Hendricks, Harper One

2. *Feel the Fear…And Do it Anyway*, Susan Jeffers Ph.D., Ballantine Books

Epilogue

1. Leaders Eat Last: Why Some Teams Pull Together and Others Don't, Simon Sinek, Portfolio, attributes it to Zen Buddhism

ABOUT THE AUTHOR

—

FOR SO LONG I thought I had to change who I was in order to fit into the world. I wanted to be seen as being the right kind of person who delivered results, met clients' needs, and never relented in order to be valued at my work.

Nothing brought this to light more than when I was working for a company that asked me to lead a sales team using the most aggressive and 'traditional' sales processes. It was the constant 'always be closing', 'mosquito-style pesky persistence' and fear-based selling that left me feeling terrible about my work and myself.

I knew there had to be a better way, a better way to connect with clients, create solutions that solved their problems, and feel good about sharing what I had to offer.

For the past twelve years, working with more than ten thousand leaders, sales professionals and entrepreneurs, from Fortune 500 to small business, I successfully developed and taught what I'd intuitively discovered. Sell From Love is built on my more than two-decade career in sales and a foundation of research that included 235 global interviews with entrepreneurs, financial advisers, coaches, consultants, and service-based professionals. I've participated in more than 800 coaching sessions, observing leaders directly coaching their sales teams and helping them improve their sales coaching skills so that their teams could sell with confidence, build client loyalty, and grow their business.

Selling from love is a business strategy unlike any other. You can be a good person, do good work, and make good money doing it. Selling from love will help you get more clients, grow your business, and make a meaningful impact on others.

I feel truly blessed and honored to have the opportunity to bring you Sell From Love so you can align your purpose and your client and offer authentically.

Now here's my formal author bio:

Finka Jerkovic is an international speaker, workshop facilitator, and leadership coach.

As President of FINKA Communications Inc., she consults with clients in areas of personal branding, leadership development, sales and marketing, client experience, and employee engagement. She brings more than two decades of experience in corporate Canada in the financial services industry, with an expertise in sales, leadership, communication, and coaching.

Finka's leadership and team development programs have been delivered to organizations across North America and Europe with a client roster that includes Lowe's, Toyota, Unum | Colonial Life, Schneider Electric, Network of Executive Women, Merck, and The Executive Institute.

Finka is the Program Director and Lead Coach for How to Fascinate® and the creator of the Certified Fascinate® Advisor program, through which she has personally trained more than one hundred and fifty advisors in using the Fascination system and tools.

She lives in Canada with her husband and daughter on their 85-acre nature oasis, where you'll find them living a farm-to-table lifestyle, brewing up essential oil blends from their lavender field, riding horses, and beekeeping.

Finka believes that when you bring authentic leadership and a mission-based mindset to business, you can achieve inner fulfillment and outer success and create a transformational impact.

HAS THIS BOOK HELPED YOU SELL FROM LOVE?

——

Could you do me a favor? I'd appreciate if you left a review online with your preferred retailer. Reviews help readers find my book, which will spread the word about the importance of selling from love. Thank you.

Want to buy multiple copies of *Sell From Love* for your leadership team, sales team, or company? Fantastic. I can help. I can also help you customize sell from love to your team or organization. You can hire me to bring the ideas of sell from love alive with your team and clients through my high-energy, interactive, live or virtual workshops, keynotes, and coaching programs.

Contact me at finka@finka.ca for more information about ordering books and customized training programs.

MAKE YOUR LEARNING LAST

▬

You don't need to go it alone. You have access to more resources and support to help you implement your ideas, stay consistent, and remain dedicated to your commitment to sell from love.

Take the Sell From Love Test at www.sellfromlove.com/test

Download the Sell From Love Workbook at www.sellfromlove/workbook

Join the Sell From Love Community at www.sellfromlove.com/community

Let's stay connected! Find me on social media:

Linked In: https://www.linkedin.com/in/finka-jerkovic-66763160/

Instagram.com/finka_jerkovic

Facebook.com/sellfromlove

Manufactured by Amazon.ca
Bolton, ON

15691832R00146